THE GREAT BRITISH
SEWING BEE

FROM STITCH TO STYLE

WENDY GARDINER

FOREWORDS BY
ESME YOUNG & PATRICK GRANT

quadrille

CONTENTS

FOREWORD BY ESME YOUNG

I am so delighted and excited to be part of the new series of *The Great British Sewing Bee*. Having worked in the fashion and film industry for many years, when I am teaching on the fashion course at Central Saint Martins in London my aim is always not only to instruct the technical side of garment construction, but also to inspire students to expand their repertoire and allow their imagination to bring out the designer in them.

Being the 'new bee' on the team could have been daunting but it wasn't, because the whole crew, and especially Patrick, welcomed me so wonderfully. It was also a huge pleasure to watch the contestants grow throughout the series, becoming bolder in their choices of fabric, more adventurous in their final projects and meeting the 90-minute challenges head on.

Of course, Patrick and I were there to find Britain's best amateur sewer and so the challenges were designed to test their skills, their technical knowledge and their ability to adapt, alter and fit a garment. As a teacher and mentor, I am used to encouraging, sharing knowledge and helping my students improve their skills, so I was delighted to see how the contestants shared this experience amongst themselves. It might have been a stressful experience much of the time, as they worked against the clock, but there was always the undercurrent of companionship and mutual love of sewing.

Sewing is fun – it is inspirational and empowering, and it is the opportunity to put a very personal stamp on an outfit, whether it is by making up a pattern in your own choice of fabric or adapting a design to suit you. The contestants in this year's Bee showed us that, even when making exactly the same garment, the choice of fabric, haberdashery and thread, results in a wonderful variety. With this book, you too have the opportunity to create your very own designs using some of the projects from *The Great British Sewing Bee* to challenge yourself.

Sewing for yourself, family and friends makes designers of us all. As the maker, you can choose what fabric you work with, whether to add or leave out elements of a garment such as pockets, collars or cuffs. Lengthen, shorten, add sleeves, mix up the colours – the choices are limited only by your imagination – so take inspiration and make something unique today.

FOREWORD BY PATRICK GRANT

It is wonderful to be back for the fourth series of *The Great British Sewing Bee* and to be working alongside the brilliant Esme, whose ideas with regards to sewing and design really resonate so strongly with my own.

It is also great to meet a new cohort of sewers. Each year I am surprised and delighted by the contestants that come on the Bee. They are always so positive, even under the most intensive of scrutiny, they never shirk the tough challenges, and the breadth of their knowledge and inventiveness must inspire so many viewers.

As with the last three series, I am always bowled over by the camaraderie in the room. Our sewers are so generous with their knowledge, they support each other technically, always sharing an insight or a bit of experience, but also, perhaps more importantly, they support one another emotionally. It is often the case that a win for one really does seem like a win for all. Sometimes it is tough to remember that this is a competition.

With this series of Bee, more than any before, we have pushed into new sewing categories. We have tackled sportswear, lingerie and clothing from Asia and Africa, most of them pieces we see around us every day but might never have stopped to look at carefully.

We have made clothes in the finest silks and the most robust wools, the sturdiest cottons and the stretchiest jersey. We have used colour, embellishment and pattern, from beautiful embroidered saris to the loudest, most beautiful Dutch wax print. We have used jacquard silks and woollen spun tweeds. The right fabric makes a garment. The right drape, the right texture, the right pattern. Sometimes simple cutting and a beautiful fabric is enough to make the most stunning piece of clothing.

From an unfamiliar cut to an undiscovered fabric, the world of sewing is very broad. I hope we will inspire home sewers to have a go at projects that they wouldn't have dreamt of trying before.

Do enjoy this book, share in some of the projects and challenges from *The Great British Sewing Bee* and try your hand at some new ideas that might just broaden your sewing skillset, but above all please enjoy.

INTRODUCTION

Dressmaking is about creating your own unique style and making something that is special to you. It is your choice of fabric and trims that enable you to make a bespoke piece – that brings out the designer in you. You can sew the same garment repeatedly, of course, changing the type of fabric to suit the season, changing the colour or pattern and making it personal and to your style every time.

As with the previous editions of *The Great British Sewing Bee* book, this one is packed with 27 projects and variations – or pattern 'hacks' – so that you can create your own wardrobe of garments as well as make for friends or family. We start with a chapter of useful guidance on getting started, covering pattern know-how, fitting tips, basic sewing and seaming, to ensure success as you progress through the projects. All the chapters have been styled to help you on your sewing journey, starting with some easy makes in the FOUNDATION chapter, before going on to INSPIRATION and then EXPLORATION where you can confidently sew with tricky and luxury fabrics, add surface decoration and make uniquely cut Japanese-inspired garments.

The projects come with full-size patterns and clear, beautifully illustrated instructions, plus plenty of tips to help you achieve professional results. In the accompanying pattern pack are full size trace-off paper patterns for every garment that requires a pattern piece. In addition, every pattern can be downloaded at www.quadrille.co.uk/fromstitchtostyle, printed off at home and then pieced together.

The step-by-step instructions for each project are headed by a materials list and layout plan for 115 cm (45 in.) and/or 150 cm (60 in.) wide fabric (where appropriate), making them easy to follow. Many of the patterns you will recognise from the TV series, including the stripy bias-cut top, babygrow, Chinese-style top, retro 1960s colour-blocked dress, asymmetric skirt, soft-cup bra, cycle top and pin-tuck shirt. You may also recognise the child's dungarees, which were featured in the series last year. These, combined with the patterns created exclusively for this book, ensure that there is something to sew for all the family.

Amongst the projects are easy-to-follow Core Skill techniques, which we hope will inspire you to attempt something new, comforted by the knowledge that help is to hand. There are also techniques to help you develop your skill set – for instance, not just one type of zip insertion, but a choice of traditional lapped zip, invisible zip, exposed teeth or surface-mounted. You can also add linings to skirts, dresses and trousers, even if a pattern doesn't call for a lining – we've provided the know-how. All this means is that you have choices: you become the designer of your very own projects, creating something that is truly unique to you.

KNOW BEFORE YOU SEW

Packed with useful information to help you sew successfully, this chapter provides essential tips and guidance to get you started. Take a look at what is in an essential sewing kit and brush up on your sewing machine basics. With advice on how to determine your pattern size, discover how to use the patterns in the book and adjust them to suit your own individual shape.

BASIC SEWING KIT
AND WISH LIST

Basic Sewing Kit

1 DRESSMAKING SHEARS AND EMBROIDERY SCISSORS – good dressmaking shears are essential. Often they have moulded handles, so if you are left-handed, look for shears designed with you in mind. Many have angled blades so you can use them easily on a flat surface. Also keep a pair of small sharp embroidery scissors to hand – very useful for clipping into small areas and snipping off thread ends.

2 NEEDLES – a selection of hand and machine needles will help to ensure success. Machine needles should be replaced regularly – after eight hours of sewing or with every new project. Ball point or stretch needles are used on knit fabrics, whilst universal sharps are used on wovens. Needles come in different strengths to suit different fabric weights – a fine needle is used for lightweight fabrics, whilst a more robust jeans needle is useful for multi-layers and thick fabrics. Generally, the higher the number on the needle, the thicker it is, so size 70/9 is for lightweight fabrics, whilst 110/16 is for heavyweight fabrics. Twin needles form two perfectly parallel rows of stitching at the same time.

3 PINS – good quality, sharp pins are essential. Glass headed pins are easy to remove as you work, can be seen if dropped and won't melt into the fabric if you inadvertently iron over them. Replace these as they become blunt to prevent them snagging the fabric.

4 THREAD – use high quality, branded thread when sewing on a machine. General purpose polyester or poly/cotton sew-all thread is perfect. Try to colour match the fabric if possible, using the same thread in the bobbin as on the top. Buy two reels per garment.

5 PATTERN PAPER – essential when creating your own patterns, making adjustments to existing patterns or to trace off the designs in this book. You can choose dot-and-cross, plain or gridded paper. The gridded or dot-and-cross versions help to ensure straight of grain, whilst the plain paper is easier to see through.

6 MARKING TOOLS – a selection of marking pens and chalks can be used to transfer marks from patterns to fabric, and to draw out cutting lines, folds, darts and buttonhole positions. Generally, mark on the reverse of the fabric whenever possible just in case they don't rub or wash off. Invest in some washaway and fadeaway pens that are easy to use when a dot is required to mark darts, for example. Never iron over marks made with pens as the heat may set them permanently. Either wait for them to fade, or wash away first.

7 QUICK UNPICK/SEAM RIPPER – this ultra useful tool usually comes with your sewing machine. It may become blunt over time, so do replace it regularly. It is used to unpick seams as well as to open buttonholes.

8 TAPE MEASURE – it is essential to measure and mark accurately; if yours is very old, consider replacing it as tape measures can stretch over the years.

9 STEAM IRON AND PRESSING CLOTH – a good steam iron and pressing cloth will help to ensure your projects look professionally finished. Always press each seam before sewing over it again. A square of silk organza is great to use as a pressing cloth because it is transparent and withstands high temperatures.

10 INTERFACING – this is applied to the reverse side of the main fabric to support and strengthen areas. It is available in different weights to suit light, medium and heavyweight fabrics, and it comes in white, charcoal or beige. It can also be fusible (iron-on) or sew-in.

11 STABILISERS – these are used to back work prior to stitching to prevent it distorting, puckering or stretching out of shape. Once stitched, stabilisers can be removed; they are availabile in tearaway and washaway types, along with heat-away versions that disintegrate when ironed.

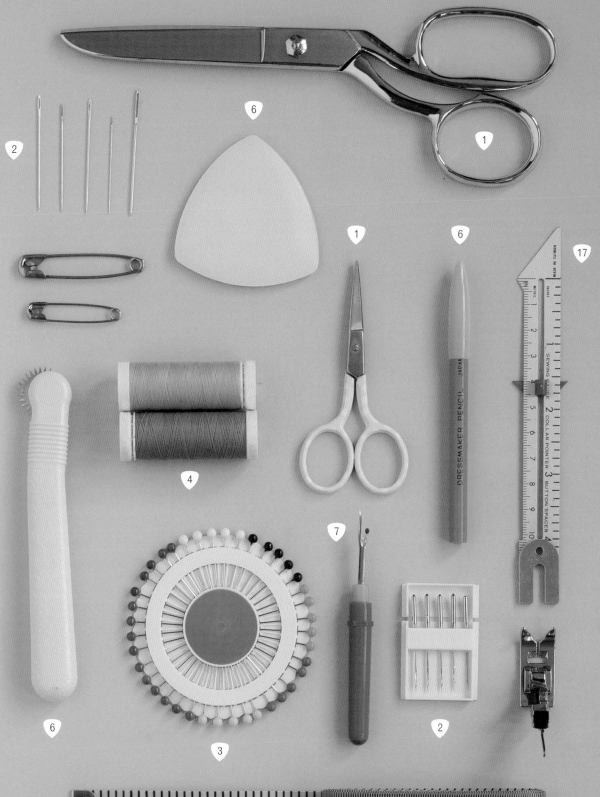

Wish List

The following haberdashery items aren't essential, but they are handy to have around:

12 PINKING SHEARS – these scissors have zigzag edges with which to cut seam allowances and prevent them from fraying without the need for other neatening techniques. They work best on lightweight cottons and felts.

13 FRENCH CURVE – a nifty ruler with a curved end and long edge, as well as a straight edge. It is useful for helping to re-shape garment pieces, such as neckline, armhole, sleeve cap, hip and waistline, if you are adapting patterns to suit your own style.

14 METRE RULE – a long, straight ruler marked in metric and imperial is useful when creating your own patterns or when straightening edges of the fabric.

15 BIAS TAPE MAKER – finishing edges with bias binding is so much easier with the use of a tape maker. They are available in different sizes or widths to create bias binding from 6 mm (¼ in.) to 5 cm (2 in.). You simply pull bias strips of fabric through the tape maker, which folds the long edges into the centre as you pull them through. Work on an ironing board and iron them as they come out the other end. Generally, the width of the strip is twice the finished folded binding, so if you want 2.5 cm (1 in.) wide bias binding, you cut strips to 5 cm (2 in.).

16 FABRIC GLUE – useful in the workbox, it can be used to stop thread tails unravelling. Also handy when clipping into V-necklines and tight corners that need to be cut close to stitching; a little dab will prevent the fabric from fraying.

17 POINT TURNER – this little tool helps achieve crisp corners. It has a point at one end for pushing out corners fully and often also has measurements marked on one side that can be used to measure and mark hem allowance and depth of pleats. If you don't have a point turner, use a knitting needle instead.

SEWING MACHINE BASICS

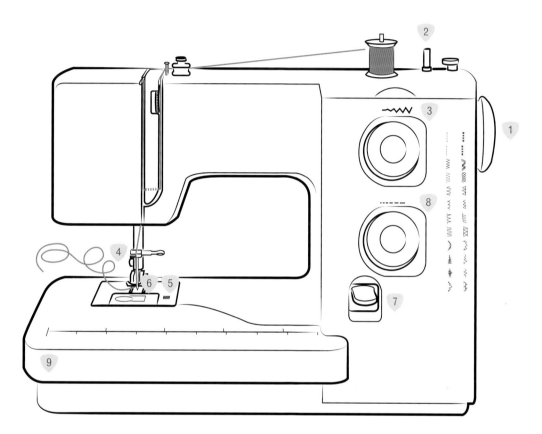

The anatomy of a sewing machine

All sewing machines work in basically the same way. They have a top thread and a bobbin thread, which interlock to create the stitching visible on the top and bottom of the fabric. All sewing machines also have the basic components in the same place.

Threading

Remember to raise the presser foot before threading to ensure the thread slips between the tension discs, then follow the thread path (which is usually numbered). Make sure you add a thread retainer disc to hold the thread spool on the spindle.

Key

1 BALANCE WHEEL

2 BOBBIN WINDING SPINDLE

3 TENSION DIAL

4 NEEDLE

5 THROAT PLATE

6 FEED DOGS

7 REVERSE STITCH LEVER/BUTTON

8 STITCH WIDTH AND STITCH LENGTH DIALS/BUTTONS

9 FLATBED/FREE ARM

1 BALANCE WHEEL – found on the upper right side of the machine, the balance wheel is used to lower and raise the needle by hand. Always turn the wheel towards yourself. On older or cheaper models of machine, there may be a separate outer ring that is pulled out a little to disengage the needle when winding bobbins.

2 BOBBIN WINDING – to wind a bobbin, place it on the winding spindle and thread, following the bobbin thread path. Most bobbins will only wind until they are full and then automatically stop. The thread on the bobbin should feel firm and look evenly wound.

BOBBIN – your machine may have a drop-in or a front entry bobbin that sits in its own case. Take care to drop in the bobbin with the thread coming off correctly, from left to right (anticlockwise). If the bobbin is inserted the other way, with the thread coming off clockwise, it may cause skipped stitches.

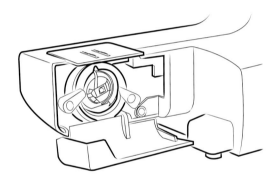

For front-loading bobbins, insert the full bobbin with the thread coming off clockwise. Pull the thread end through the gap in the casing to pull it through the bobbin tension and then insert the casing into the front of the machine.

3 TENSION – the thread and needle tension is set by a dial on the front or top of the machine, normally just above the needle area. It is numbered and will usually have the most common or default tension highlighted in some way – by darker numbers or circled numbers. Generally, leave the tension set at the default position as most modern machines stitch perfectly well on all types of fabric. If you do adjust the tension, do so a little at a time. Perfect stitches are formed when the top thread is visible only on the top of the fabric, and the bobbin thread only on the underside.

4 NEEDLE – machine needles have a flat section on the shank, which is usually placed 'flat to back' of the machine when fitted up into the needle socket. Tighten the screw holding the needle in place with a screwdriver (from the tools provided) to prevent it working loose as you sew.

5 THROAT PLATE – this has markings to show different seam allowances, as well as the central holes through which the feed dogs rotate and the needle goes to pick up the bobbin thread.

6 FEED DOGS – under and protruding through the throat plate are the feed dogs – the gripper teeth that rotate to help move on the fabric under the presser foot as it is stitched.

7 REVERSE STITCH – all machines will have a lever or button on the front of the machine; most have to be held down to continue stitching in reverse and, when released, will then revert to forward stitch.

TIP

Always use bobbins intended for your make and model of machine; although they may look the same, sometimes they are very slightly different in size and thus fit.

TIP

Start sewing about 1 cm (⅜ in.) from the fabric edge, take three or four stitches, then hold down reverse and backstitch to the fabric edge, before continuing forward. This will fix the stitching and prevent the fabric from tangling or being pulled into the feed dogs at the start.

**8 STITCH WIDTH AND STITCH LENGTH DIALS/
BUTTONS** – these are used to alter the width and
length of the selected stitch. A standard length for
most purposes is 2.2 to 2.5. Use a longer stitch for
multi-layers or bulky fabrics. Stitch width is used for
all sideways stitches (zigzag or decorative stitches).
The higher the number or wider the printed scale, the
longer or wider the stitch.

TIP

On most machines the needle
position can be altered when straight
stitching by pressing/turning the
stitch width button/dial. This means
you can control where stitching
is placed, and use the presser foot
edge as a guide.

9 FLATBED/FREE ARM – all machines have a 'flat
bed' – the surface area around the needle that helps
to hold fabric flat as it is sewn. Most convert to 'free
arm' by taking part of the flat bed away. The part that
can be removed may be clipped to the front, the back

or wrapped around front, back and side. It frequently
holds the tools tray too. Converting to free arm gives
you a narrow section that exends above the worktop,
which means you can stitch small areas such as
cuffs, sleeves and trouser legs more easily.

Added extras

As machines increase in price, so they increase
in functions and facilities. Many of the additional
features are conveniently sited just above the needle
area, so are close to hand when sewing. These can
include a fix/lock stitch button, a sewing speed lever,
a stop/start button to use instead of a foot pedal and
a knee lift lever.

Machine maintenance

Make sure you change your needle every eight hours
of sewing, or after every project – particularly when
sewing tough fabrics or multi-layers.

Defluff the machine after every project by removing
the bobbin and using the little brush provided to
sweep out the fluff. Occasionally you should also
unscrew and remove the throat plate, remove the
bobbin holder and brush out underneath. It gets
surprisingly dirty.

Many modern sewing machines are self-lubricating
so you don't need to oil them. However, they do still
need maintenance and service.

WHAT PATTERN SIZE AM I?

One of the main reasons to make your own clothes is to get garments to fit properly, so the first step is to choose the correct pattern size. To do that you need to take accurate measurements. Never assume you are the same size pattern as you are ready-to-wear.

Measuring

To achieve the best results when measuring it is important to measure over the undergarments you normally wear.

- -

TIP

Enlist the help of a good friend or partner. It is far easier to take accurate measurements for someone else.

- -

Hold the tape measure comfortably snug, but not tight. Then measure:

1 **HEIGHT:** standing against a flat wall without shoes, from the floor to the top of your head.

2 **BUST:** around the fullest part of the bust and straight across the back.

3 **HIGH BUST/CHEST:** directly under the arms, straight across the back and above the bust.

4 **WAIST:** if not obvious (and as we get older, it often isn't!), tie a narrow elastic or string around your middle and bend slightly from side to side to allow it to settle naturally at your waistline. Measure over the elastic. Keep the elastic in place for the next measurement.

5 **BACK WAIST LENGTH:** from the most prominent bone at the nape/base of neck to the natural waistline.

6 **HIP:** around the body at fullest part, usually 18 to 23 cm (7 to 9 in.) below the waist.

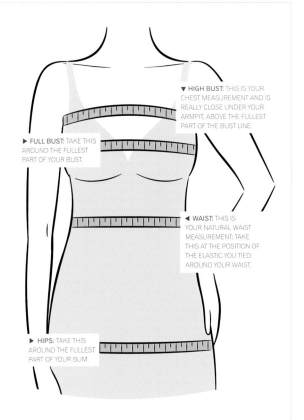

▼ **HIGH BUST:** THIS IS YOUR CHEST MEASUREMENT AND IS REALLY CLOSE UNDER YOUR ARMPIT, ABOVE THE FULLEST PART OF THE BUST LINE.

▶ **FULL BUST:** TAKE THIS AROUND THE FULLEST PART OF YOUR BUST.

◀ **WAIST:** THIS IS YOUR NATURAL WAIST MEASUREMENT; TAKE THIS AT THE POSITION OF THE ELASTIC YOU TIED AROUND YOUR WAIST.

▶ **HIPS:** TAKE THIS AROUND THE FULLEST PART OF YOUR BUM.

The bust, waist and hip measurements are used to determine your pattern size. Note that you may very well be a different size pattern for bust, waist and indeed hip. This is quite normal – very few people are the perfect pattern size. But with multi-sized patterns you can quite easily cut from one size cutting line to another and back again.

Choosing your size

DRESSES, TOPS, JACKETS

If you have more than 6.5 cm (2½ in.) difference between bust and high bust, select your pattern size by HIGH BUST measurement). You will then need to alter the pattern to fit the fuller bust, but it should fit better across shoulders, chest and torso. For pattern alteration tips, see pages 23–27.

SKIRTS AND TROUSERS

Use your waist measurement unless your hips are two sizes or more larger than your waist, then use your hip measurement.

BETWEEN TWO SIZES

For a closer fit or if you are small boned, select the smaller size. For a looser fit or if you are big boned, select the larger size.

Most female patterns are designed for a woman who is1.65 m to 1.67 m (5 ft 5 in. to 5 ft 6 in.) and male patterns for a man who is 1.78 m (5 ft 10 in.). If you are taller or shorter, you may have to adjust the pattern length (see page 23).

Make a note of the pattern sizes you are closest to but do check regularly by re-measuring yourself, particularly when starting on a new project in a luxury fabric.

STANDARD READY-TO-WEAR WOMEN'S MEASUREMENT CHART

UK DRESS SIZE	8	10	12	14	16	18	20
BUST (cm)	83	88	93	98	104	110	116
BUST (in.)	32½	34½	36½	38½	41	43¼	45½
WAIST (cm)	65	70	75	80	86	92	98
WAIST (in.)	25½	27½	29½	31½	33¾	36¼	38½
HIP (cm)	92	97	102	109	113	119	125
HIP (in.)	36	38	40⅛	42¾	44½	46¾	49¼

STANDARD READY-TO-WEAR MEN'S MEASUREMENT CHART

UK SIZE	34	36	38	40	42	44
CHEST (cm)	86.5	91.5	96.5	101.5	106.75	111.75
CHEST (in.)	34	36	38	40	42	44
WAIST (cm)	71	76.5	81.5	86.5	91.5	97.5
WAIST (in.)	28	30	32	34	36	38¼
SEAT (cm)	86.5	91.5	96.75	101.5	106.75	112
SEAT (in.)	34	36	38	40	42	44⅛

MY MEASUREMENTS	CLOSEST PATTERN SIZE TO MY MEASUREMENTS		
	BUST	WAIST	HIPS
HIGH BUST			
FULL BUST			
WAIST			
HIP			

USING THE PAPER PATTERNS

We have included 27 projects in this book, most of which have a full-scale, multi-size pattern printed on the pattern sheets. The pattern pieces are overlaid across one another so you will need to trace off the pieces you want to use. Of course, tracing them means the originals are left intact and can be used and adapted time and time again in different sizes too.

Use dressmakers' tracing paper, which is see through and is available in packs containing large sheets suitable for big pattern pieces. Other paper, such as dot-and-cross or baking parchment paper, can be used but may have to be pieced together first.

Spread out the pattern sheet that includes the pieces you need. Lay the tracing paper on top, smoothed flat and anchored in place with weights (tins of beans work beautifully).

Having selected your size, trace around the cutting line for each piece in your size.

Unique sizing

If you need to blend one size into another, because you are different sizes on the bust, waist and hips, do this as you trace off the design. If, say, you are a size 14 bust but 16 waist and 18 hip, trace the fullest size from hip down, trace the bust from 14 up and then blend the lines from hip to waist and waist to bust. A French curve helps with this as the curve on the ruler enables you to easily draw the new cutting line. Alternatively, dot between the lines and then join the dots.

- -

TIP

If you like a pattern but it includes a detail, such as welt pockets, that you are unsure of – leave them out. That is the beauty of making your own garments.

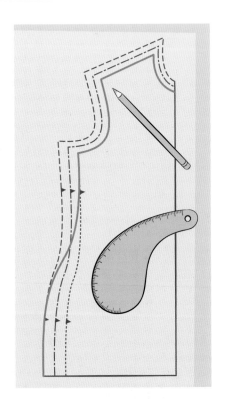

THIS ILLUSTRATION SHOWS PART OF THE PATTERN PIECE FOR THE BACK OF A FITTED DRESS IN THREE SIZES – 10, 12 AND 14. THE BLUE LINES ARE THE PATTERN LINES FOR EACH SIZE; THE RED LINE IS OUR HAND-DRAWN LINE ON THE TRACING PAPER, SHAPING THE DRESS FROM A SIZE 10 AT THE BUST, THROUGH A SIZE 12 AT THE WAIST AND A SIZE 14 AT THE HIPS.

Pattern markings and terminology

Patterns are full of useful markings, dots, lines and arrows that are all included to help with the cutting out and construction of the garment. Once you understand what each of the symbols or lines mean, you will quickly learn to read the pattern and will find putting the garment together so much easier.

GENERAL INFORMATION – each pattern piece includes the pattern number, sizes on that particular piece, what the piece is (e.g.. FRONT), and simple cutting directions such as, 'CUT 2 FABRIC, CUT 1 INTERFACING'.

GRAINLINE ARROWS – usually these will have arrowheads at one or both ends. These lines are pinned parallel to the selvedge to ensure the pattern piece is correctly angled and cut out.

ANGLED GRAINLINE – 'place to fold' lines have a right-angled arrowhead at either end to indicate that the pattern piece should be put on the fold of fabric.

CUTTING LINES – the outside lines on the pattern pieces are the cutting lines. Different sizes have different line types such as solid, dotted or dashed, which are also numbered by size. In some areas the lines merge, so it is advisable to go over your size line with a coloured pencil before tracing.

NOTCHES – these are triangular symbols shown on the cutting line extending into the seam allowance. These are used to match up seams, front to back, sleeves to armholes. Cut these notches outwards from the cutting line so the seam allowance remains intact in case it is needed to tweak the fit. You will then use them to match garment pieces.

LENGTHEN OR SHORTEN LINES – are two parallel lines that indicate where the pattern can be made longer or shorter without distorting the garment shape.

SOLID LINES WITHIN THE PATTERN – these indicate buttonhole positions and may also indicate the location of bust line, waist line and hip line.

CIRCLES – these are used to mark the ends of openings such as zips, or the end of stitch lines such as gathers. They also mark placement of details such as darts, tabs, belt loops and pockets.

CIRCLE WITH A CROSS THROUGH IT – this symbol marks the main fitting line on the body, at the bust, waist and hip. Sometimes on commercial patterns, the finished garment measurements are printed alongside this symbol.

DARTS – are shown as V-shaped broken lines with dots. To sew, match the dots, folding fabric with right sides together and stitch along the broken line from widest point to tip. Darts shape fabric to fit over body contours.

PARALLEL LINES WITH CIRCLES AND AN ARROW LINE AT THE BOTTOM – indicate positions of tucks and pleats. One line is the fold line, the other the placement line. Sometimes these are differentiated by a broken line and a solid line. The arrowhead indicates which direction to take the fold. To make pleats, fold the fabric on the solid line and bring fold to broken line, then press. Baste across the top of pleats to hold in place.

GET SET TO SEW: FROM TRACING PATTERNS TO CUTTING OUT

Once you have traced off the pattern pieces required for your chosen garment, you will need to put the pieces on the fabric, and cut and mark them ready for construction. Follow these tips to ensure success.

Fabric layouts

Each of the projects in this book has a pattern layout to follow, but as a general rule you will find that most pattern pieces are cut out from fabric that has been folded in half lengthways, with selvedges together, so that you cut two matching pieces from each pattern piece. This makes it quicker, and ensures you get two perfectly matched pieces.

The fabric is folded, right sides together so that any markings can be easily transferred from the pattern to the wrong side of the fabric.

Check against the specific layout plan to ensure the pieces are all correctly laid out and pinned in place before cutting out. Before removing the pattern piece from the fabric, transfer any markings (see opposite). Once markings are transferred, remove pins but keep the pattern piece folded with the fabric so you can refer to it when making up the garment.

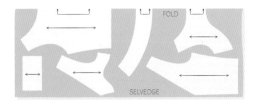

Alternative fabric layouts

Sometimes it is necessary to cut out pieces from fabric that is folded widthways or from single layers due to the size of the pattern pieces. For instance, a wide circular skirt piece will be wider than a fabric that has been folded lengthways so the fabric may be folded widthways, which keeps the width of the fabric as it is. Note the selvedges will therefore be opposite each other rather than folded together.

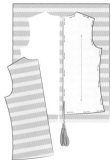

Another option is to cut from a single layer – useful when cutting from a patterned fabric that requires careful alignment so the fabric design matches across seams, or to avoid prominent motifs falling awkwardly. When cutting from a single layer, you will need to flip the pattern piece over to cut the second piece in order to get a right- and left-hand pair.

The all important grainline

It is very important that the grainlines are parallel to the selvedges of the fabric in order to ensure that pattern pieces are cut out accurately and will not have unwanted stretch in odd areas. Matching the grainline will also help prevent twisted or rippling seams.

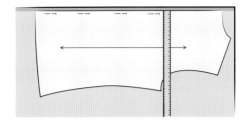

To ensure that pieces are placed properly, position the pattern piece on the fabric according to the layout plan but, before pinning it, measure from the selvedge to the grainline at one end. Pin the pattern in place, then measure from the other end of the grainline to the selvedge. Adjust the pattern if necessary so that it is the same distance as the first end. Once correctly positioned, pin the rest of the pattern to the fabric.

Remember that some pieces should be placed on the fold of the fabric, indicated by a grainline with right-angled arrowheads. Placing a piece on the fold means that you will cut a single piece, which when unfolded is perfectly symmetrical. First pin the pattern to the fold, keeping the straight edge straight along the fold, and then pin in place.

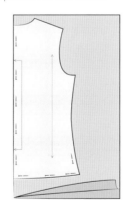

Pinning and cutting out

Having matched grainlines to selvedges, pin around the pattern pieces, pinning just within your cutting line through the pattern and both layers of fabric. Take care that the fabric doesn't crease or crumple up; avoid leaning too heavily on the fabric. An alternative to pinning is to hold the paper pieces in place with weights. There are purpose-made dressmaking weights, or you can use stones or even tins of beans.

To cut the pieces, use good quality dressmaking shears, keeping the blades running along the table as you take long cuts. Cut out around the notches.

Transferring markings

The pattern pieces have lots of useful information and markings to help with construction. Some of these need to be transferred to the fabric to match pieces and to correctly place pockets, darts, pleats and zips. Marking pens and chalks are the perfect tools. Test out pens on a scrap of fabric to ensure the mark can be removed and that it doesn't 'bleed' into the fabric.

NOTCHES – these should have been cut outwards around the pattern pieces However, if you have missed one, mark the placement of notches by snipping into the seam allowance a little.

DARTS – you will need to transfer the circle marks for the dart onto the fabric. A super quick method is using a pin and marking pen or chalk pencil.

1 Make a tiny hole in the paper at the circle placements, then use a chalk pencil or marking pen to dab a dot through the hole on the top layer of fabric (remember you are working on the wrong side of the fabric). Repeat for all the circles of the dart.

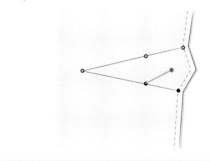

2 Insert a pin in the holes through both fabric layers, lift the fabric to reveal the bottom layer and mark fabric at the pins.

Marking with tailor's tacks

If you are sewing delicate fabrics, sheers or those on which the chalk/pen marks won't show, mark positions with thread markings called tailor's tacks.

1 Thread a needle with double thread and make a stitch through the circle, through the pattern and both layers of the fabric, leaving at least 2.5 cm (1 in.) thread tail.

2 Make a second stitch at the same spot, leaving a long loop in the stitch. Cut the thread with a long thread tail.

3 Snip into the loop, then gently pull the fabric layers apart and snip the threads in the middle so that some thread is on either piece of fabric.

Pinning to sew

It is now time to remove the pattern pieces and prepare to sew. As you pair up the garment sections, it is advisable to anchor them together to hold the seam straight and prevent layers 'walking' or misaligning as you guide them through the sewing machine. To do this either pin baste or thread baste/tack.

PIN BASTING

Pin basting is a quick method. On most seams it is advisable to place the pins at right angles to the seams so you can whip them out as you get to them (avoid sewing over pins, which may break or bend the machine needle).

You can also place pins vertically down the seamline, which can help to keep the seam straight and hold the fabric layers together securely. Again pins need to be removed before you get to them. Place the pins so they are pointing towards the machine needle and the heads are nearest you to make them easier to remove. Use this method for trickier areas such as sleeve insertion or zip insertion.

THREAD BASTING/TACKING

Thread basting or tacking is an alternative to pin basting. It does take longer but is preferred by some as it holds layers together very securely and enables you to try on the garment if required. To baste, starting with a knot and using a contrasting thread colour and double thread, hand stitch big stitches that can be removed once the seam is sewn. To remove basting, snip off the knot at the start, cut into stitching at regular intervals and pull out the threads.

Baste next to the seamline, just inside the seam allowance, to make the threads easier to remove once the seam is stitched.

FIT TIPS

We sew our own garments because we want clothes that are unique and fit correctly. But few of us are 'standard' sizes and, indeed, most of us will be different sizes for bust, waist and hips. The good news is that many fitting adjustments are simple to make.

Wearing ease

Nearly all garments will have some 'ease' built into the pattern so that there is room to move, sit and walk. (Those that don't provide ease include corsets, which are often made slightly smaller, and close-fitting Lycra garments such as swimwear). The amount of ease depends on the garment – more is included in coats and jackets than in blouses and dresses – and what the designer envisages. To determine the amount of ease that is incorporated into a garment, compare the Finished Garment Measurements with the Size Chart Body Measurements. The difference is the amount of wearing/designer ease that has been included.

Take a similar existing garment that fits you well and turn it inside out and lay it flat. Pin the pattern pieces to the garment, matching shoulders, centre front and so on to get a sense of how well the new pattern will fit. You can quickly alter your pattern just by pinning a little here and there till it matches the contours of your favourite dress or trousers.

Most female patterns are designed for someone who is 1.65 m to 1.67 m (5 ft 5 in. to 5 ft 6 in.) tall and is a B cup with proportional bust, waist and hips. As only 25 per cent of women fit this standard, some adjustments to patterns will be necessary for most of us.

Wherever possible, pattern fit first, remembering to pin out seam allowances, darts, tucks and pleats. Pin one front to one back along the shoulder and side seamline and try on the half garment. Check the bust dart is in the right place, and that the side seams, centre front and centre back are aligned. At this point it is easier to add or deduct pattern paper or move the bust point.

Following are the most common fitting adjustments.

Altering the length

If it is necessary, this is the first adjustment to make, before altering width or bust point. Most patterns for dresses and trousers will have a lengthening and shortening line. If there isn't one, you can adjust the length by adding or shortening at the hemline. To determine whether you do need to lengthen the garment pieces, measure your back length from nape of neck to hemline and check it against the pattern piece.

TO LENGTHEN

Cut between the two parallel lengthening and shortening lines and spread the pattern pieces apart by the amount you need to lengthen. Slide a piece of pattern paper underneath and tape it in place. Make sure you line up vertical lines such as the grainline. If necessary, use a pencil and ruler to redraw the outside edges into a smooth line.

TO SHORTEN

Fold the pattern along the lengthening and shortening lines, making a tuck in the pattern piece that is half the amount by which you would like to shorten the garment. For example, if you want to shorten by 4 cm (1½ in.) make a 2 cm (¾ in.) tuck. Pin or stick down the tuck.

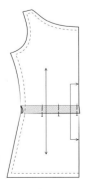

Moving bust darts

As women get older, so their bust point moves south. The bust point is the fullest part of your bust. Check whether the bust point on the pattern is in line with your own figure. If not, you can move it up or down quite simply.

1 Use a ruler and pencil to draw a rectangle around the bust marking. Cut out around the box and then slide it up or down as required, keeping the cut edges parallel.

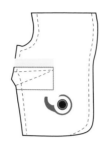

2 Stick the box into its new position and fill the space with some pattern paper. Use a ruler and pencil to match up and redraw the outside lines.

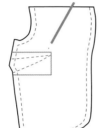

Full or small bust adjustments

As most patterns are cut to a B cup, many of us need to make a full bust adjustment (FBA) if bigger or smaller than a B cup. Whilst it can seem daunting, it does make a difference to how the garment will fit and once the technique is mastered, it becomes second nature.

There is no exact formula to work out how much of an adjustment you need, as it will vary depending on the garment you are making. For instance, a very loose fitting top with lots of ease may not need adjusting, whereas a fitted dress will.

To make any adjustment easier, first you need to select your correct pattern size. To do this, take your bust measurement and your high bust measurement. The first is taken around the fullest part of the bust, straight across the back. The second taken above the bust under the arms, straight across the back.

If the difference between the two measurements is more than 6.5 cm (2½ in.) choose your pattern size for dresses, tops, jackets and coats by your high bust measurement (see page 17 for size charts). This will ensure a better fit through neck, shoulders, chest and torso with just the full bust adjustment necessary.

Examples of measurement variations are below.

The process of adapting a pattern for both a full bust adjustment and a small bust adjustment (SBA) is the same, except for the FBA you cut and spread the pattern pieces and for the SBA you reduce by overlapping the pattern pieces.

	EXAMPLE 1: FBA	EXAMPLE 1: SBA	MY MEASUREMENTS
FULL BUST MEASUREMENT	97 cm (38 in.)	89 cm (35 in.)	
HIGH BUST MEASUREMENT	89 cm (35 in.)	86.5 cm (34 in.)	
DIFFERENCE	8 cm (3 in.)	2.5 cm (1 in.)	
FBA = half the difference	4 cm (1½ in.)		
SBA = half the difference		1.25 cm (½ in.)	

Full bust adjustment steps

1 Hold the pattern paper against yourself, matching the shoulder seamline to the top of your shoulder. Check the bust point and if necessary move the dart as noted opposite in Moving Bust Darts.

2 Using a ruler and pen, draw a vertical line from the bust point on the pattern to the hemline, making sure the line is parallel to the grainline. From the top of this vertical line, draw a diagonal line up towards the armhole, hitting the lower third of the armhole (or the armhole notch if one is provided). These two lines are now called Line 1. Draw a second horizontal line through the centre of the bust dart from side seam to bust point. This is Line 2.

3 Cut along Line 1 from the hem up to the armhole, but leaving a small join or hinge at the armhole so you can pivot the paper. The point of the dart can now swing away from its previous position. Cut through Line 2 through the middle of the dart, again leaving a little hinge of paper at the tip of the dart so you can pivot the pattern paper.

4 Align the cut edges of Line 1 to spread them apart by half the amount of your FBA, keeping the vertical lines parallel to each other. As you do this, the dart will spread

and become bigger and the lower edges of your hem no longer meet at the bottom as the adjusted side is now longer. To correct this, draw another horizontal line parallel to the bottom edge and cut along it to spread the pieces apart until your hem is level. Fill in all the spaces with spare pattern paper and tape in place.

5 ADJUSTING PATTERNS WITHOUT DARTS
If your pattern does not have a bust dart, you can make the FBA by creating your own dart. Measure up from the waist 15 cm (6 in.) along the side edge and

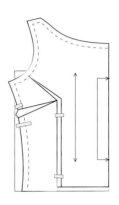

mark with a dot. Draw a straight line from this mark to the bust point on the pattern. Again draw a straight line from the lower third of the armhole to the bust point and then from there down to the lower edge, as before. Slash and spread the pattern paper by the required amount, add extra pattern paper and tape in place. Now to close up the side opening created, draw a dart equal to the width of the side opening with the tip of the dart 2.5 cm (1 in.) from the bust point. Lengthen the centre front as noted above.

SMALL BUST ADJUSTMENT STEPS
This is the same process as the FBA but in reverse. Draw in the lines and cut along them as for the FBA adjustment above. Pivot the darted side of the pattern across the other side by the desired SBA amount. The lower edges of the hem no longer meet as the side adjusted is shorter. Cut along the third line drawn to move the pattern piece until the hem is level.

Adjusting the back

If you find that your clothes gape or strain at the back it could be because you have a broad or narrow back and adjustments can be made to ensure a better fit. This is the beauty of dressmaking, we don't have to put up with ill-fitting clothes or buy bigger.

1 NARROW BACK
Draw a vertical line down from the shoulder, starting 3 cm (1¼ in.) from the armhole and ending just below the bottom of the armhole. Draw a second line out to the side of the pattern at a right angle from the bottom of the first line.

2 Cut along the two lines to separate the piece and slide it over towards the centre back, overlapping the paper. Generally around 6 mm (¼ in.) is enough but you can play around with this distance to suit your own needs. Stick the pattern paper in place. Use a ruler and pencil to redraw the side seam into a smooth line.

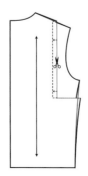

3 Check the resulting shoulder length and adjust the shoulder length on the front pattern piece accordingly. Note if you take in more than just 6mm (¼ in.) you may have to adjust the sleeve head of a sleeve.

1 BROAD BACK
Draw the lines as in step 1 for a narrow back, and cut out the section.

2 Instead of overlapping the pattern pieces, spread them apart. Again there are no set rules, but a 6 to 13 mm (¼ to ½ in.) adjustment is usually sufficient. Fill in the space created with some pattern paper and stick the pieces together. Use a ruler and pencil to match up and redraw the outside of the side seam.

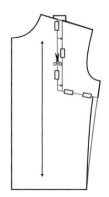

3 Again you will need to adjust the shoulder length of the front pattern piece, making it a little longer to match the back.

Fitting trousers

There are a few common adjustments that will improve the fit for most of us.

CROTCH DEPTH

The crotch depth and length are very important in making trousers. Crotch depth is the distance between your waist and the crotch line on the pattern and is what defines the rise of your trousers. It can  vary enormously between women. To measure this, sit on a hard chair and measure the distance from your waist to the seat. Check your measurement against the waist to crotch line on the pattern (remember to measure from the seamline at the waist).

The process of adjusting the crotch depth is basically the same as lengthening and shortening a dress or skirt (see page 23). Draw a horizontal line across the trouser pattern along the hip line and add the required amount of extra paper to lengthen, or fold a tuck if you need to shorten.

CROTCH LENGTH

The crotch length is the measurement taken from the front of the waist, between your legs to the back waist.

(see page 23)

TIP

If you are using luxury fabric, make a 'toile' first. Baste darts and all seams together. Check for fit and make any adjustments by tucking, or cutting and slashing.

---

1 ADJUSTING CROTCH LENGTH
Compare your measurement to the curved crotch seam on the pattern and if different, divide the difference by half.

2 With both front and back trouser pieces on a flat surface, mark a point 8 cm (3 in) below the waistline on both crotch seams. Draw a horizontal line from this mark to the side seam on both pieces. Cut along the lines, leaving a hinge at the side seams.

TO INCREASE THE CROTCH LENGTH

Spread the pattern apart by the amount needed, hinging at the side seams. Fill in the gap with pattern paper and tape in place.

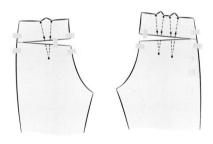

TO REDUCE THE CROTCH LENGTH

Overlap the pattern pieces at the crotch by the desired amount and tape in place.

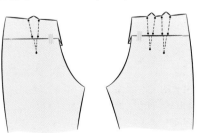

COMMON SEWING TERMS AND TECHNIQUES

As with any hobby, there are certain terms and techniques that become second nature – once you are familiar with them. To help you avoid confusion when reading a pattern or trying a new project, we've included the most frequently used terms in a handy A to Z listing.

BACKSTITCH/ REVERSE STITCH – sewing machines have a button or lever to reverse the direction of the stitching. This

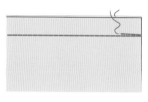

is used to anchor stitches at the start and end of a seam. It is best to start about 1 cm (⅜ in.) from the fabric end, stitch forwards for three or four stitches, and then hold the button or lever to reverse to the fabric end before continuing forward.

BASTING/TACKING – stitching used to temporarily hold fabrics together. You can tack by hand or machine – on a machine, set the stitch length to the longest possible so that it will be easy to remove later.

BIAS CUT – the bias of the fabric has the most 'give' and is most stretchy. The true bias of a fabric is diagonally across the weave at a 45-degree angle to the selvedge. Even if a garment is cut on the 'straight of grain' there may be elements that are on the bias, such as shaped or V-necklines, which need to be handled with care. Prevent unwanted stretch with staystitching.

COUCHING – is a technique for attaching thicker threads to the surface of the fabric to embellish. You

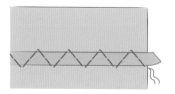

can couch all sorts of yarns, ribbons or thick threads, using a triple-zigzag stitch. Reduce the width of this stitch so that the right and left swing is just off the edge of the trim.

EASING/EASE STITCH – this is a slightly longer straight stitch used to very slightly gather fabric so that it can be eased into a smaller piece, or on a curved hem. Ease stitching is used to attach set in sleeves, to join

princess-seamed pieces and to help take up hems on circular skirts without leaving ripples. To ease stitch, increase the stitch length to 4 and sew just within the seam allowance (on sleeve heads, sew again 3 mm (⅛ in.) from the first row). Pull up the stitching to gently gather the piece until it fits smoothly into the other or, in the case of the hem, turns under neatly.

EDGE STITCHING – this is the same as topstitching and is meant be visible on the surface of the fabric, but it is sewn much closer to the edge, hence its name. It is used to attach pockets, etc.

FACINGS – these are used to neaten and finish off the edges on necklines, armholes and waists instead of collars, sleeves and waistbands. They are interfaced to add support and attached right sides together before being turned to the inside.

GATHERING – can be done by machine or hand. On a machine, set to the longest stitch length and start at one end, leaving a long thread tail. Then stitch just inside the seamline, leaving long thread tails. Pull up the bobbin thread from either end to gather the fabric, moving the gathers along evenly. On a long section, split the length into sections and gather individually. To gather by hand, use double thread and take long running stitches, pulling up the fabric as required.

GRAINLINE – it is very important to follow grainline markings on dressmaking patterns. The grain is the warp and weft woven fibres in the fabric. The lengthwise grain (or 'warp') runs down the fabric parallel to the selvedges and is the most stable

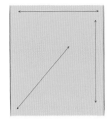

and least stretchy. The crosswise grain (or 'weft') runs across from selvedge to selvedge. Most pattern pieces will have grainlines marked on them, which need to be aligned parallel to the selvedge on the 'straight of grain' to prevent the garment pieces twisting or hanging lopsided. Measure from the grainline on the pattern to the selvedge at each end of the line.

INTERFACING – this is used to add support and stability to areas that need extra strength, such as collars, cuffs, waistbands, facings and button positions. See page 35 for more information.

PRESSING – always press seams before they are sewn over again. Pressing embeds the stitches and helps the seam lie flat. Press from the wrong side and then the right side, protecting the fabric with a press cloth.

RIGHT SIDE/WRONG SIDE – fabrics have a 'right' side, which is the pretty printed side that will be visible as the outside of the garment, and a 'wrong' side, which is the reverse. If the fabric is a solid colour and it is difficult to tell the right side from the wrong, mark each piece you cut out with a chalk cross on the 'wrong' side so that you put the pieces together accurately. Sometimes, a very slight shade variance may be visible in daylight.

SATIN STITCH – this is used to cover the edges of an appliqué or create defined stitched lines. It is made from a very close zigzag stitch. To achieve it, reduce the stitch

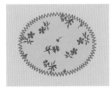

size to approximately 0.3 to 0.5 in length and the stitch width to 3.5. Test it on a scrap of fabric to determine the best combination of width and length.

SEAM ALLOWANCE – this is the distance between the stitching and the fabric edge. The amount needed depends on the project but generally, for dressmaking it is 1.5 cm (⅝ in.), for crafts 1 cm (⅜ in.), and for patchwork 6 mm (¼ in.). It is important is that you are consistent and

use the same seam allowance within a project and, when following a pattern, use the seam allowance noted in the instructions.

SELVEDGES – these are the side edges of the fabric piece. They are often woven slightly tighter than the rest of the fabric, so shouldn't be included in a pattern piece as they may cause a seam to twist. Align the grainline on the pattern with the selvedge to ensure the piece is cut out accurately.

SLIPSTITCH – a hand stitch often used to close up openings left to turn through fabric, instead of ladder stitch, or for hemming. First tuck the raw edges of the opening inside, then working on the fold of the fabric, slip the needle through the fold about 6 mm (¼ in.) along. Come out and pick up two or three threads of the fabric on the opposite side, slide through the opposite fold again, and repeat along the opening.

STAYSTITCHING – a row of straight stitching, made just inside the seam allowance on areas that you don't want to stretch out of shape while you are working on them. To staystitch, sew with a

regular stitch length just within the seam allowance. You will need to staystitch areas that are cut on the bias, such as necklines and curved princess seams. On necklines, stitch from the shoulder towards the centre from both shoulders to prevent stretching.

TOPSTITCH – this is stitching that is visible on the surface of the project. It can be sewn with a straight stitch or a decorative stitch. Topstitched hems are

usually sewn about 1 cm (⅜ in.) from the edge. Where possible, use the edge of the presser foot as guide when topstitching to ensure straight even lines.

UNDERSTITCHING – this is used to anchor the seam allowance to the facing, which helps to ensure the facing stays

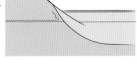

inside without rolling out after it is turned to the inside. To understitch, first sew the facing to the garment, right sides together, then press facing and seam allowances away from the garment. With the facing uppermost, sew close to the seam on the facing, catching the seam allowances underneath as you sew.

HELPFUL HAND-SEWING STITCHES

Arming yourself with a few simple hand stitches is sensible because, although most dressmaking is done by machine, there are occasions when sewing by hand is easier, dare I say, quicker, and more efficient.

Running stitch

Ideal to repair a burst seam, gather fabric or baste/tack something in place. Thread a needle and knot at the end. Bring the needle to the surface from the wrong 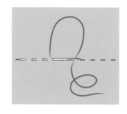 side of the fabric, and then slide your needle in and out of the fabric three or four times along the stitching line taking even stitches of about 6 mm (¼ in.) in length with even gaps.

Backstitch

Use to hand stitch seams together. Thread the needle and knot the end. Starting from the wrong side of the fabric, bring the needle to the front about 1 cm (⅜ in.)  from the end. Take the needle to the reverse of fabric back behind the first position by about 6 mm (¼ in.), bringing it up again in front of the first position by 6 mm (¼ in.). Repeat, taking the needle to the reverse back by the first stitch. The stitches will then slightly overlap on the underside but look continuous on the right side.

Herringbone stitch (catch stitch)

This is a great stitch for hand sewing hems, and works extremely well on thick fabrics such as 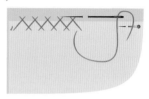 wool or gabardine when a single turned hem allowance is used.

Neaten the raw edge of the hem allowance using zigzag or overedge stitch and turn up the hem. Start by knotting the thread and anchoring the knot underneath the hem allowance on the left side (the stitch is created from left to right). Make a diagonal stitch up to the right and catch just one or two threads from the garment above the hem with the needle going into the fibres horizontally from right to left. Bring the needle diagonally down to the lower right and catch a deeper amount of the hem allowance. Again take the needle up to the right into the garment, taking a horizontal stitch through one or two fibres towards the left. Bring the needle back down to the hem allowance to the right. Continue in this manner around the hem. Finish with a couple of stitches on the spot in the hem allowance.

Button sewing

1 Take a length of cotton or poly/cotton sewing thread as long as your arm. Without cutting it, pull off another equal length.

2 Fold this extra-long piece of thread in two and thread the folded end through a needle, pulling through until all ends are even. There are now four strands of thread on the needle. Knot the four ends together.

3 Start from the right side of the garment where the button is to be sewn, take the needle to the underside so the knot will sit out of sight below the button. Bring the needle back up to the front close to the knot and through the button above the knot.

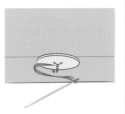

4 Position a spent match or cocktail stick on top of the button, between the holes. Then take the thread to the underside through the opposite hole, but going over the stick. Repeat a couple more times.

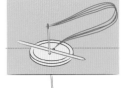

5 Remove the stick and take the thread to the underside of the button, but still on right side of the fabric. Pull the button away from the fabric and wrap the thread around the loose strands holding the button in position to create a shank. Wrap about four or five times, leaving enough to tie off.

6 Take the needle to the underside and tie off by taking the thread through itself twice and pulling tight. Cut the thread.

Slipstitch

Used to close turning gaps or sew double-turned hems. Anchor a knot inside the fold of the hem, pick up a tiny thread from the garment fabric and then pass the needle back into the folded hem allowance. Slide the needle forwards inside the fold by about 1 cm (⅜ in.), then bring it up and through a tiny thread of the garment again. Continue like this to complete the hem. On the right side of the garment all that should be visible is a tiny prick stitch and on the reverse, a small V-shaped stitch.

Ladder stitch

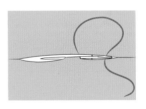

Very similar to slipstitch, this is used to close gaps left to turn through items. Start with a knot slipped inside on the lower folded edge, then bring the needle up through the fold into the fold of the upper edge. Slide the needle along the fold by 1 cm (⅜ in.) and bring it back out and into the lower folded edge. Again slide the needle along a little before bringing it up and through the upper fold. Continue this method to close the gap completely.

FIT AND STYLE SOLUTIONS

Most of us can be categorised into one of five shapes. Which shape are you?
Check the descriptions below to determine which silhouette best describes
you and then choose garments that flatter your figure.

Rectangle or 'athletic'

If your figure is straight up and down without a lot of curves, you fall into this body-type classification.

STYLE TIP: Create curves to flatter your figure – wrap-over styles work well for your shape, creating a nipped-in waistline. Choose styles with defined waistlines or two-piece outfits. Most skirt shapes will suit your figure. Try a peplum skirt, such as the Peplum Dress on page 104.

Triangle or 'pear'

The most common female silhouette, this is where the upper body is noticeably smaller than the lower body.

STYLE TIP: Since the waist is your best feature, choose styles with a defined waistline. The Chinese-Inspired Top on page 148 is perfect for your shape. Alternatively, try the Jumpsuit on page 56.

Inverted triangle

When shoulders are wider than the hips, you have an inverted triangle shape. You may also have a small waistline.

STYLE TIP: V-neck tops work well for your figure as they minimize the width at the bustline. Try the Bias-Cut Top on page 38. Balance out the upper half with an elegant flared skirt or trousers. Try the Palazzo Pants on page 138.

Apple

If you have a full figure with the upper body, especially the tummy, bigger than your lower half, you have an apple-shaped silhouette.

STYLE TIP: Fluid lines up and down the body work well for apple shapes as there are no seamlines drawing the eye. The Jersey Dress on page 100 is a perfect style that you will wear again and again.

Hourglass

The hourglass shape is curvy, with a clearly defined waist.

STYLE TIP: Wear belted dresses, skirts, tops or jackets to define the waist. Why not try the Wiggle Skirt on page 112.

Style it yourself

The beauty of sewing for yourself is that there are no rules. Wear patterns and colours that make you happy and feel confident. If you love tropical prints, then use them. If plain colours are your thing, then play with some colour blocking. Unlike shopping on the high street, you are the designer when you make your own clothes. So have fun... and start sewing!

CHOOSING FABRICS

One of the pleasures of dressmaking is that we get to choose the fabrics and colours we want to wear. But of course, it can be a little daunting if you don't know what type of fabric to use or whether special sewing techniques are needed. So we've put together a basic guide to fabrics with tips on how to sew them successfully.

Building a swatch book

Most of us buy fabric on impulse and add it to our stash without necessarily having a garment in mind. And then when we want to make something, we buy more, or spend hours going through the hoard to find something suitable. So, whenever you buy fabric, cut a small swatch from it and add it to a notebook, with details of what it is, and how much you bought. Not only will this be helpful when you wish to make something on the spur of the moment, it will also help you to build a library of fabric types.

Suitability of fabric

As well as buying a fabric because you love it, you do need to consider its suitability for the projects you have in mind. An embroidered medium-weight denim would be lovely as a fitted dress or A-line skirt, but not good for a flowing blouse that needs to drape and flow. Equally, floaty chiffon is unsuitable for a pencil skirt – unless (and there are always ways around things) you use it as a top layer, with an underskirt in something more stable and opaque.

To start with, it is advisable to choose the fabric types that are recommended with the patterns. This way you know they will work. Check the design detail on the pattern, such as gathers, pleats or tucks, and feel the fabric, does it drape easily or will it hold pleats, for example.

Fabric types

There are three main categories: woven, knit or stretch, and non-woven fabrics.

WOVEN FABRIC – these are quite simply woven with warp and weft threads. Woven fabrics include woollens, gabardine, chiffon, voile, cotton, polyester, silk, linen and denim. They come in different weights to suit different needs, from thick mohair, Melton or tweed woollens for coats and jackets to lightweight chiffon, silk and polyester for blouses, lingerie or over-dresses.

KNIT OR STRETCH FABRICS – these are made from fibres that loop around one another to create the cloth. It is the looping of the threads that gives the cloth the stretch or flexibility. Stretch fabrics can be made from different fibres or a mix of fibres, which will affect their stretchability. Different types of stretch fabric include knits, which look as if they have been hand knitted, to double-knit jersey, single knit (lightweight and fine), or those mixed with polyester or viscose. For tips and technique for sewing with stretch fabrics, see pages 103 and 176.

NON-WOVEN FABRICS – these include cloth made by matting or pressing fibres together, such as felt or fleece, or man-made PVC, faux leather and suede. Interfacing is often a non-woven fabric also.

Linings, interlinings and interfacing

As well as the main fabric needed for garments, you may want to add linings, interlinings and interfacing.

LINING – this is a second layer of fabric on the inside of a garment. Linings can be silky, to help you to slip the garment on and off easily, or can made from a fine cotton or a heavier satin in jackets and coats. A favourite for dressmakers is an anti-static lining that allows the body to breathe. Linings are often cut from the same pattern pieces as the main garment, but without facings, waistbands or collars. For more on linings, see page 134.

INTERLINING – this is another layer used to provide support and stability, usually on specific areas of the garment such as collars, cuffs, and upper chest in coats and jackets or in formal dresses. It is often cut from the same fabric as the rest of the garment and sewn around the edges to the wrong side to create a double layer, which is then treated as one piece. An interlining may be included as well as a lining.

INTERFACING – this is used to add support and stability to certain sections of a garment, such as facings, waistbands, collars and cuffs. The idea of interfacing is to add support without changing the 'handle' of the fabric – or the way it drapes. You can use purpose-made interfacing or another layer of your main fabric if you prefer. For example, a delicate chiffon blouse might need interfacing down the front to support the buttonholes but, if you don't want it to show, you might use another layer or two of fashion fabric instead. Throughout the projects in this book, we advise on what interfacing to use.

For more information on interfacings and interlinings, see page 54.

Preparing fabric

Fabrics should be pre-shrunk before you start dressmaking with them. This is very important, particularly when lining a garment, as the lining may not shrink in the same way as the main fabric. Some fabrics require washing twice before use, so do check care requirements.

For washable fabrics, put through the washing machine and then hang to dry naturally. Press carefully to reset the grain before cutting out. For delicate fabrics such as silk, wash by hand and air dry. You can double check whether it is essential to hand wash the garment by machine washing a small 10 cm (4 in.) square of fabric. Allow to dry, then press and check whether it has shrunk. With dry-clean-only fabrics, you don't necessarily have to dry clean them before use, but you do need to check whether they will shrink with steam.

WOOLLENS – hover the steam iron over the fabric using lots of steam. Allow each section to cool before moving it as when warm it can stretch. Repeat this for both sides of the fabric.

SILKS – the lustre of silk can be destroyed with too much pressing so do test a small piece to see how it responds to heat and steam. Always press from the wrong side and use a pressing cloth to protect the surface.

LACE OR MESH FABRICS – it is easy to accidently distort lacy fabrics so treat them like wool. First test a small piece to make sure that the heat doesn't melt the lace, just hovering the iron over the cloth with some light steam. If it is OK, continue on the whole piece.

FABRICS WITH METALLIC THREADS – again test a small piece. Avoid steam initially as the moisture and heat in steam may shrink the metallic threads more than the threads they are mixed with. Once the temperature is right, and the test piece doesn't shrink, you can try introducing a little steam.

LEATHER AND SUEDE – generally avoid ironing these fabrics. If you do need to, make sure you cover the fabric with a good pressing cloth and test the temperature on a scrap first.

CHAPTER ONE

FOUNDATION

Build on your knowledge by making some staple garments with simple lines and basic techniques. The garments in this chapter are all easy pieces to get you started. Choose from a stripy bias-cut top, a child's A-line skirt, a lined and hooded cape, a babygrow, a unisex kimono and a jumpsuit with an exposed zip. Alongside the projects are core skills features that enable you to master specific techniques – from seam finishes to appliqué embellishments – and use them on any other project of your choosing.

BIAS-CUT TOP

BIAS-CUT TOP

This bias-cut top is a wardrobe staple. Team it with skirts, trousers or jeans for a more casual look. The pattern is fairly simple and will take you through how to work with fabric on the bias. It's a handy skill to learn and once you understand the concept of working on the diagonal grain of fabric, you can create skirts and dresses with beautiful draping. This project also shows you how to match stripes to create a striking chevron pattern.

MATERIALS
1.5 m (1⅝ yd) fabric 150 cm (60 in.) wide

Matching sewing thread

Basic sewing kit (see page 10)

DIFFICULTY LEVEL
Beginner/Intermediate

FABRIC SUGGESTIONS
Georgette, crepe de chine, viscose, or floaty lightweight cotton types like voile or lawn, polyester, silk and silky fabrics.

DESIGN NOTES
This is a simple top with centre front and back seams so that a stripey fabric can be cut and joined with a chevron effect down the front and back. The neck is bound with a fabric strip and the armholes have a single-turned hem. Of course, if you are a newbie, you can make this top from a plain fabric and avoid having to match stripes!

Use a 1.5-cm (⅝-in.) seam allowance throughout, unless otherwise stated.

FINISHED MEASUREMENTS	8	10	12	14	16	18	20
BUST (cm)	89	94	99	104	110	116	122
BUST (in.)	35	37	39	41	43¼	45⅝	48
WAIST (cm)	85.5	90.5	95.5	100.5	106.5	112.5	118.5
WAIST (in.)	33⅝	35⅝	37⅝	39⅝	41⅞	44¼	46⅝
HIP (cm)	94.5	99.5	104.5	109.5	115.5	121.5	127.5
HIP (in.)	37¼	39⅛	41⅛	43⅛	45½	47⅞	50⅛

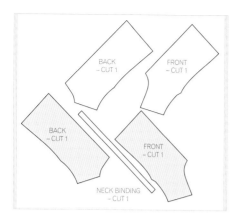

LAYOUT PLAN

Trace off the pattern pieces – front, back and neck binding. After preparing your fabric, lay it out as a single layer, with the right side facing up. Lay out the pattern pieces on the bias – at a 45° angle – as shown. Keep the grainline on the pattern parallel to the selvedge. Pin and cut out one front and one back piece, and the binding. Then, to ensure the chevron stripes match, turn the back and front pieces over, matching up the stripes, and cut the second front and back. Transfer markings to the fabric (see Get Set to Sew, page 21).

1 Staystitch (see page 29) the front and back neck edges 13 mm (½ in.) from the edge by stitching with a regular 2.5 stitch length just inside the seam allowance, sewing from the side edges to the centre.

TIP

If you are using a lightweight or sheer fabric hand tack the seams first, using a 1-cm (⅜-in.) seam allowance, before machine stitching.

2 With right sides together, pin and sew the centre front seams, carefully matching the stripes as you pin. Neaten the raw edges together, then press the seam to one side. Repeat for the back panels.

TIP

If you are using a lightweight or sheer fabric, the finish will be neater if you use French seams (see page 42).

If you are cutting this out in a lightweight or sheer fabric, pin the fabric to a layer of pattern paper then lay the pattern pieces on top and cut out through all three layers to stop the fabric from moving.

TIP

Press the closed seams flat, then them press over to one side. Pressing the stitches flat first "sets" them.

3 With right sides together, pin and sew the front to the back at the shoulder seams. Neaten the raw edges together and press the seams towards the back. With right sides together, pin and sew the side seams. Neaten the seams together, as before, and press the seams towards the back.

5 Pin mark the quarter points around the neckline of the top, using the centre front as the starting point.

6 Aligning the raw edges, matching the seam in the neck binding with the centre back seam and all four quarter points on the binding and neckline, pin the binding to the neckline. Fill in the spaces with pins, and stitch with a 1-cm (⅜-in.) seam allowance. If necessary, clip into the garment neck edge to make the binding fit smoothly. Trim the seam allowance to 6 mm (¼ in.).

4 ATTACH THE NECK BINDING

Fold the neck binding strip in half widthways, right sides together, and pin and stitch across the short ends to join the strip into a loop. Press the seam open. Fold and press the strip in half lengthways, wrong sides together, and mark the quarters with pins.

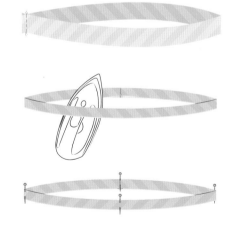

7 Working from the wrong side, turn and press the folded edge of the binding to the inside of the garment. Pin in place and edge stitch close to the folded edge.

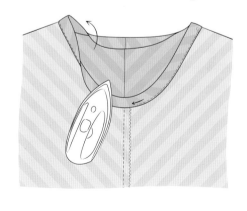

CORE SKILL
Simple seams and seam finishes

SIMPLE SEAMS

STRAIGHT STITCH SEAM

The most common dressmaking seam, with the fabrics sewn right sides together at an equal distance from the fabric edge – usually 1.5 cm (⅝ in.). For light- to medium-weight fabrics, use a stitch length of 2.2–2.5. For heavier, thicker fabrics increase to 3. Backstitch at start and finish of the seam.

STRETCH STITCH SEAM

Most machines will have one – use for all horizontal seams when working with stretch fabrics. Alternatively, a small zigzag stitch will work, too – simply reduce the stitch width to 2.5–3 and the stitch length to 1.5–2.

NARROW SEAM

This is used for transparent and lacy fabrics. Sew a regular straight stitch seam and then sew again with a tiny zigzag stitch if the fabric may fray (or a straight stitch if not) close to the seam line. Trim the seam allowance close to the second stitching.

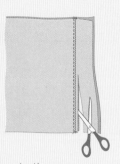

FRENCH SEAM

Great for transparent fabrics or when the inside of a garment may show. First sew the seam with the

WRONG sides of the fabric together, taking a scant 6-mm (¼ in.) seam allowance. Trim this to 3 mm (⅛ in.), then turn the fabric through, with the RIGHT sides together and the seam right on the edge. Press. Stitch with a 1-cm (⅜-in.) seam allowance.

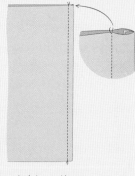

FLAT FELL SEAM

Useful for reversible items, or to give added strength. Sew with the wrong sides of the fabric together. Press the seam allowances to one side and then trim the under seam allowance to a scant 3 mm (⅛ in.). Fold the edge of the upper seam allowance under by 6 mm (¼ in.), overlapping the under seam allowance. Stitch in place through all layers. Lengthen the stitches for the second row of stitching for the thicker fabric layers.

LAPPED SEAM

Ideal for fabrics that don't fray and for yokes and small areas in woven and knitted fabrics. On non-fraying fabrics, trim the seam allowance on the upper piece. For woven and knitted fabrics, fold along the seam line on the upper piece. Lap the trimmed or folded edge onto the seam line of the other piece of fabric. Hold the layers together with pins, tacking or with a fusible tape or glue. Stitch close to the lapped edge. If required, add a second row of stitching 6 mm (¼ in.) away. Press.

SEAM FINISHES

OVERLOCKING

The overlocking stitch is formed of either three or four threads and neatly encases the raw edges. A four-thread overlocker  will sew a straight stitch to the left, with a second straight stitch to the right, anchoring the two looper stitches that form over the edge of the fabrics interlocking together. As you feed the fabric through the machine, a cutter trims the excess seam allowance before the stitching covers it.

OVERCAST/OVEREDGE STITCH

If you don't have an overlocker, you can use the overedge or overcast stitch, which has a straight stitch to the left with a zigzag going over the edge to the right. It is sewn on the edge of the fabric to neaten the seam allowances. Most machines come with an overcast foot.

ZIGZAG STITCHING

This can be used to neaten the raw edges of seam allowances either individually or together. Once the seam is sewn, change to zigzag stitch and sew again in the seam allowance.

HONG KONG STYLE (BOUND)

This finish is ideal when the inside of the garment might show, as the seam allowances are neatly bound. You can use bias-cut strips of lining fabric or organza or a special seam binding tape. Press the seam allowances open and then wrap a bias strip around the seam allowance. Sew it in place with a straight stitch, stitching through the seam allowance and the bias tape only.

CLIPPING/NOTCHING CURVED AREAS

When a seam allowance is inside collars, cuffs, facings, waistbands or hem allowances, the raw edges need finishing to help them lie flat when 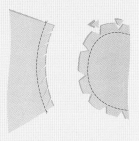 the fabric is turned through to the right side. Inner curves should be snipped into the seam allowance diagonally, and outer curves notched with little wedge shapes.

CLIPPING CORNERS

To create crisp corners, stitch the pieces together, reducing the stitch length to 2, about  3 cm (1¼ in.) from the point, take one stitch diagonally across the point, and then stitch for 3 cm (1¼ in.) before increasing the stitch length again to a regular 2.5. Trim quite close to the stitching about 2.5 cm (1 in.) along either seam towards the point. At the point, trim diagonally across the seam allowance.

GRADING SEAM ALLOWANCES

To eliminate bulk and prevent a bulky ridge from forming, cut the seam allowance that lies closest to the outside of the garment to 6 mm  (¼ in.) and the under seam allowance to a scant 3 mm (⅛ in.).

See page 44 for further tips on seams.

8 HEM THE TOP

Neaten the raw edges of the armholes, then press under a single 1-cm (⅜-in.) hem and machine stitch in place. Hem the bottom of the top in the same way.

SEAMING TIPS

No matter what seaming method is used, there are a few tips that make sure the seams are smoothly stitched without puckers and pulls.

- Test before best! Before stitching a seam, test stitch using the same combination of fabric and interfacing layers. Try out different stitch lengths – 2.5 for light- to medium-weight fabrics, 3 for medium- to heavyweight fabrics, and 3.5–4 for heavy and thick fabrics.

- Avoid twisting and rippling seams. Stitch all seams in the same direction – i.e. from hem to top.

- Start well. Prevent fabric from being pulled into the feed dogs (into the hole of the needle plate) by starting the seam at least 1 cm (⅜ in.) from the fabric end for two to three stitches, then reverse stitch back to the end before going forwards again. This will also lock the stitching in. Reverse stitch at the end of the seam, too. If fabric still gets pulled into feed dogs at the start of a seam, add some tissue or paper underneath the seam area and/or try a finer needle size.

- Prevent 'bird nesting'. Avoid threads tangling together at the start of the seam (which can pucker fabric or just look unsightly) by holding both needle and bobbin thread taut in your left hand as you start to sew. Hold until at least 2.5 cm (1 in.) has been sewn.

- Be aware of seam allowances. Make sure they remain the same throughout the garment construction (if you are using a paper pattern, check what the seam allowance is). Generally, garments have a 1.5-cm (⅝-in.) seam allowance, whereas crafts projects have 6–10 mm (¼–⅜ in.).

- Hide thread tails. At the end of seams, take both threads to the back of the work, hide the thread tails by feeding them between the fabric layers within the seam allowance, pull taut and snip off so that they disappear into the seam allowance.

- Neaten or finish all seam allowances to prevent fraying and to reduce bulk in seamed areas (Seam Finishes, page 43).

- Press all seams before crossing over them with more stitching. Press first from the wrong side to embed the stitching and then from the right side.

CORE SKILL
Hemming

The choice of hemming method will depend on your personal preference, fabric type and project being hemmed, but whatever method is used, first you need to prepare the hem allowance.

PREPARING THE HEM ALLOWANCE

The hem allowance adds weight to the hem and helps it hang nicely. For instance, an A-line skirt in lightweight cottons needs only a little hem allowance of 2.5–5 cm (1–2 in.), while medium-weight straight skirts, dresses, jackets and trousers benefit from a larger hem allowance of up to 8 cm (3 in.).

1 Preferably hang the garment for 24 hours prior to hemming, which will allow the fabric to settle and even drop if it is cut on the bias. You can then straighten the hem edge before neatening and hemming.

2 Mark the hem level from floor upwards, placing pins parallel to the hem line.

TIP

When marking hem levels, make sure the person for whom the garment is being made is wearing the appropriate underwear and shoes, as this affects how the garment will hang.

3 Working on a flat surface, with the garment turned wrong side out, fold up the hem at the marked hemline, matching the side, centre back and front seams. Place pins vertically, removing the horizontal pins.

4 Decide on the hem allowance and mark the upper limit (the hem allowance needed depends on the project, fabric and fullness – see above). Trim the hem allowance even if necessary.

5 Finish the raw edge of the hem allowance prior to stitching the hem in place by overcasting or zigzag stitching close to the edge and then trimming close to stitching. Fabrics that do not fray, such as stretch knits and fleece, do not need neatening.

DOUBLE-TURNED TOPSTITCHED HEM

A double-turned topstitched hem is often used on lightweight cotton clothes, stretch tops etc. The hem allowance is folded over twice at the hem edge, effectively tucking the raw edge inside.

It can be achieved in two ways. You can either fold up the hem by half the required amount and then again by the same amount, which folds the raw edge under. Or you can fold up the entire hem allowance and then tuck the raw edge inside.

Press and topstitch close to the inner fold of the turned-up hem. Generally you

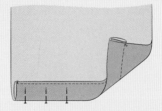

will be working from the wrong side of the garment, so make sure that the bobbin has thread to match the fabric. If desired, stitch again, working in the same direction close to the hem edge to provide two parallel lines of stitching.

TIP

Make the hem stitching a feature of the garment by using a contrast thread colour or decorative stitch.

TWIN NEEDLE TOPSTITCHED HEM

A twin needle has two needles on one shank and can be used in most machines. They are available with different width gaps between the needles, ranging from 1.6 mm (1⁄16 in.) to 6 mm (1⁄4 in.) and in different weights, such as fine 70/9 up to jeans needles 100/16, as well as in universal sharps, ballpoint and stretch varieties.

For hemming, a gap of approx 3–4 mm (about 1⁄8 in.) is ideal. On the top you will get two perfectly parallel rows of stitching, and on

the underside a zigzag-looking stitch as the bobbin thread switches between the top threads. It is therefore essential that you sew from the right side of the garment. The results look like the hems you frequently see on high-street garments.

VERY FULL OR CURVED HEMS

On circular skirts and full A-line skirts that have a curved hem, it is usually necessary to ease in some of the excess hem allowance before turning up the hem.

1 First prepare the hem allowance, as in steps 1–5 opposite.

2 Next, ease stitch 6 mm (1⁄4 in.) from the raw edge. To ease stitch, increase the stitch length

to 4–5. Then gently pull up the stitching (using the bobbin thread) and turn up the hem allowance. The slight ripples and gathers should be in the hem allowance only, leaving the garment edge smooth and ripple free.

3 Turn the raw edge under again to tuck it inside the hem allowance and topstitch it in place.

TIP

It is much easier to turn up a hem with the help of a friend. However, if you are working alone, a gadget called a skirt marker, with chalk puffer, is a great for marking hems on skirts and dresses. You set the height required with the right-angled marker that swivels on the pole and then, as you turn slowly, you can use the hand-held puffer to puff out a fine chalk line at the required hem height.

A·LINE

SKIRT

A-LINE SKIRT

This little A-line skirt for young girls is a perfect starter project, or a quick-and-easy make when time is short. It consists of just two pieces, and has a semi-elasticated waist at the back and a mock band at the front.

MATERIALS

80 cm (32 in.) medium-weight cotton, denim or twill fabric, 115–150 cm (45–60 in.) wide

30 cm (12 in.) buttonhole elastic, 18 mm (¾ in.) wide

2 buttons, 15 mm (⅝ in.) in diameter (for waistband)

4 or 5 buttons, 2.5 cm (1 in.) in diameter (for skirt front)

Co-ordinating sewing thread

Matching machine thread

Contrasting machine thread for topstitching

2 large safety pins (to insert elastic)

Basic sewing kit (see page 10)

DIFFICULTY LEVEL

Beginner

FABRIC SUGGESTIONS

This simple A-line style can be made in a variety of fabrics, from cottons, denim and linen for spring and summer to cords, flannel and fleece for winter. If you are using fleece or cords, stitch with a regular seam and neaten in your preferred manner (see page 43).

DESIGN NOTES

The side seams are French Seams (see page 42), which eliminates the need to neaten them. The hem is double turned and topstitched. If you are using a non-fraying fabric, you can turn the hem allowance under once and topstitch it in place. The back waist is elasticated, making the skirt easy to pull on.

AGE in years	4	5	6	7	8	9
WAIST (cm)	55.5	57.5	60	62.5	64.5	67.75
WAIST (in.)	21¾	22⅝	23⅝	24⅝	25⅜	26⅝
LENGTH (cm)	31	33.5	36	38.5	41	45
LENGTH (in.)	12 3/16	13 3/16	14 3/16	15⅛	16⅛	17¾
WIDTH AT HEM (cm)	82	84	86.5	89	91	94.25
WIDTH AT HEM (in.)	32¼	33	34	35	35¾	37⅛

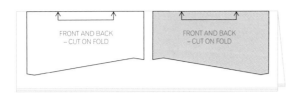

FRONT AND BACK
– CUT ON FOLD

FRONT AND BACK
– CUT ON FOLD

LAYOUT PLAN

Fold the fabric right sides together and place the pattern piece right side down on top of the fabric, with the straight edge against the fold as shown. Cut out, then flip the pattern piece over so that it's right side up and position it again the fabric against the fold. Cut the second piece out. Transfer the button positions and fold line for the waist casing from the paper pattern to the fabric (see page 21).

2 CREATE A MOCK FRONT BAND

Find the centre of the skirt front by folding the fabric piece in half and pin marking at the waist and the hem. Then make a mark 1.5 cm (⅝ in.) either side of the centre pin at the waist and hem. Using a fabric marker pen or tailor's chalk, draw in stitching lines connecting the top and bottom marks. Topstitch (see below) along the marked lines.

1 MAKING UP THE SKIRT

Staystitch the top edge of the front and back pieces (stitch just inside the seam allowance with a regular 2.2–2.5 stitch length), sewing from the side edges to the centre. Staystitching is permanent, although it will not be visible in the finished garment.

TIP

Topstitching just means the stitching will show on the right side of the garment. Remember: if you are stitching from the wrong side, it is the bobbin thread that will be visible on the outside of the garment

Use a contrast thread colour so it stands out, perhaps picking out a colour from the fabric pattern.

3 MAKE BUTTONHOLES IN BACK WAISTBAND

On the back skirt piece, make a buttonhole at each side, 2 cm (¾ in.) from the top edge and 4 cm (1½ in.) from the side seams (see page 214). These buttonholes will be in the casing when the fabric is folded down later. If you are using a thin fabric or a fabric with stretch, put a small piece of fusible interfacing over the area where you will be making the buttonhole, on the wrong side of the fabric.

4

Place the skirt front and skirt back wrong sides together, matching the side edges. Taking a scant 6-mm (¼-in.) seam allowance, sew from waist to hem. Trim the seam allowance to just 3 mm (⅛ in.) and turn through so that the right sides are together. Press, with the seams on the edge.

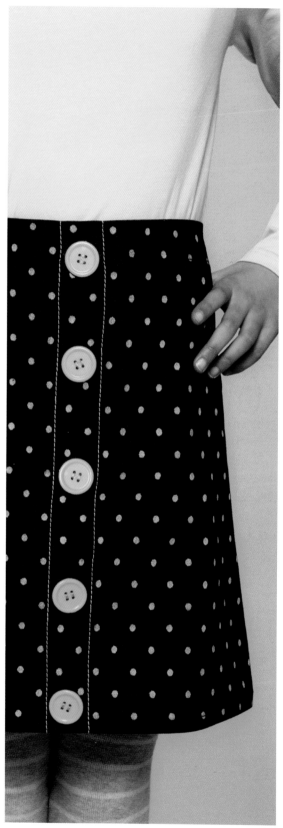

5 Sew the side seams again, this time taking a 1-cm (⅜-in.) seam allowance; this will neatly encase the raw edges of the seam allowance. Press again.

6 Neaten the raw edge of the top of the skirt by zigzag stitching close to the edge, overedge stitching (see seams and seam finishes, pages 42–43), or turning 1 cm (⅜ in.) to the wrong side.

7 STITCH THE CASING
Turn the top edge under by 4 cm (1½ in.) to form a casing and press. Stitch around the turned-under casing close to the neatened edge.

8 Stitch buttons to the back waistband between the buttonhole and the side seam, taking care that the stitching does not go through to the right side of the skirt.

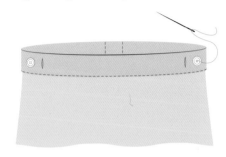

9 Attach the safety pin to one end of the buttonhole elastic. Feed it through one of the buttonholes, across the back of the skirt, and out of the other buttonhole, making sure the free end doesn't disappear inside the casing. Fasten one of the buttonholes in the elastic over one of the buttons and try the skirt on the child. Pull up the elastic to fit and attach a buttonhole in the elastic to the button on the other side.

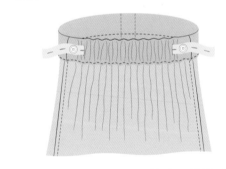

10 HEM THE SKIRT

Turn up the 2-cm (¾ in.) hem allowance and press. Tuck the raw edge inside by 1 cm (⅜ in.), so that it meets the fold; press and pin. Topstitch close to the inner fold. Press.

11

Finish the skirt by hand sewing the buttons, evenly spaced, down the mock front band. (See page 31 for a super-quick method of button sewing.).

CORE SKILL
Interfacings

Interfacing is an extra layer that is added to the reverse of some areas in a garment to add body, firmness or help support concentrated stitching without changing the way the garment drapes and hangs.

TYPES OF INTERFACING

There are three main categories. NON-WOVEN interfacing is made from pressed fibres with a felt-like appearance, there is no grainline to follow so pattern pieces can be placed in any direction. It adds firm support, even in lightweight varieties. WOVEN interfacings have a fabric grain and are handled in the same manner as fabrics. They are more flexible than non-woven types. KNITTED interfacings have two-way stretch in order to move like knitted fabrics, adding support without changing the handle of the garment.

Interfacing may be iron-on (fusible) or sew-in. It can be super-light, light, medium or heavyweight (generally, the weight used should be the same as the fabric).

TIP
On very lightweight, transparent fabrics, instead of a traditional interfacing you can use an extra layer of the main fabric, which doesn't spoil the transparency of the fabric.

APPLYING INTERFACINGS
IRON-ON (FUSIBLE) INTERFACING
While this can be quick to apply, it is very important to fuse it completely to avoid it 'bubbling' under the fabric when laundered – a problem that can't then be rectified. Iron-on interfacing is attached with a combination of heat, moisture and pressure. It has a glue applied to one side, which can be seen as a slightly raised surface that may glisten or shine.

1 Cut interfacing to the size of the pattern pieces. If you are using medium to heavyweight fabrics, trim the interfacing so that it fits just within the stitching line.

2 Place the fabric wrong side up on the ironing board with the interfacing glued side down on top. Cover with a damp cloth.

3 Check the manufacturer's instructions to find out what temperature to set your iron to and whether steam is applicable. Place the iron on top of the press cloth and press down in the same position for 10–15 seconds. Lift the iron, move to an adjacent area and press down again. Repeat until the whole area has been pressed.

4 If the corners of the interfacing can be lifted away, press again until it has completely bonded. Leave to cool completely before working with it.

TIP
The actual time to achieve a good bond varies depending on interfacing and fabric weight. Always test on a sample first.

SEW-IN INTERFACING
This is either hand or machine sewn to the reverse of the main fabric. It is the best choice for fabrics where the heat and moisture would damage the fabric.

1 Use the appropriate pattern piece to cut out the interfacing.

2 Stitch it to the reverse of the main fabric section, just inside the seam allowance.

3 To reduce bulk, trim away excess interfacing, cutting the corners at an angle.

TIP

Apply sew-in interfacings to the garment, not the facings, so that they will shadow-proof the seam allowances showing through and help prevent facings from rolling out.

SPECIALIST TAPE

There are some areas in a garment that can stretch out of shape while the garment is being constructed, such as bias-cut, round or V-necklines or shoulder seams on stretchy fabric. These areas can be staystitched (see page 29) or have a specialist tape fused to the seam line to prevent the unwanted stretch.

BIAS TAPE

This tape will bend around curves because it is bias cut, which makes it ideal for fusing to the seam allowance and on seamlines around armhole edges or necklines.

EDGE TAPE

This is a narrow strip of interfacing reinforced with stitching to add stability. Use this tape in bias-cut areas that are not supposed to have too much give – for instance, shoulder seams or skirt slits. It is applied to the seam-allowance area.

TIP

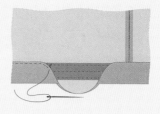

Use edge tape within the hem allowance when blind stitching by hand. Apply it to the wrong side of the main fabric and then take stitches from the edge tape only, not the main fabric. This will ensure a completely invisible hem.

WAISTBANDING

Waistbanding is useful for waistbands, front bands and pleats. It is made from non-woven interfacing and is usually fusible. Slotted banding has three lines of slotted holes, one down the centre and two either side parallel to the long edges. This makes them easier to fold in half and to stitch to the main fabric. Stiffened bandings include petersham and curved petersham.

HEMMING TAPE

Hemming tapes are strips of fusible web that melt completely to glue fabric layers together as an alternative to sewing a hem. They are also useful for anchoring ribbons to the surface of a fabric prior to stitching.

JUMPSUIT

JUMPSUIT

A jumpsuit is a comfortable, easy-to-wear garment that can be worn day or night. For day, wear it with small heels and co-ordinating accessories; for evenings, parties or special occasions, add killer heels, a statement necklace and clutch bag.

MATERIALS

3.6 m (4 yd) fabric 115 cm (45 in.) wide or 3.1 m (3⅜ yd) fabric 150 cm (60 in.) wide

70 cm (¾ yd) iron-on interfacing

45-cm (18-in.) open-ended zip

50 cm (20 in.) bias binding, 12 mm (½ in.) wide

50 cm (20 in.) elastic, 6 mm (¼ in.) wide

Safety pin

Matching sewing thread

Basic sewing kit (see page 10)

DIFFICULTY LEVEL

Beginner/Intermediate

FABRIC SUGGESTIONS

Crepe, satin back crepe, medium-weight cotton and linen.

DESIGN NOTES

This jumpsuit has a partially elasticated waist for comfort and a fashionable exposed zip at the centre front. Darts provide shaping and there are in-seam pockets at hip level. If you prefer, you can simply leave out the pockets for a smoother hip line.

Use a 1.5-cm (⅝-in.) seam allowance throughout, unless otherwise stated.

FINISHED MEASUREMENTS	8	10	12	14	16	18	20
BUST (cm)	107.5	112.5	117.5	122.5	128.5	134.5	140.5
BUST (in.)	42¼	44¼	46¼	48¼	50½	53	55¼
WAIST (cm)	83.25	88.25	93.25	98.25	104.25	110.25	116.25
WAIST (in.)	32¾	34¾	36¾	38⅝	41	43⅜	45¾
HIP (cm)	95.25	100.25	105.25	110.25	116.25	122.25	128.25
HIP (in.)	37½	39½	41½	43⅜	45¾	48⅛	50½

CORE SKILL
Elastic casings

Elastic is often inserted into a casing or stitched to the fabric edge at the same time as a casing is made in order to provide a comfortable fit at the waist.

TIP

To determine how much elastic to use, measure around the waist and deduct 2.5 cm (1 in.) for a snug fit. Rather than overlap the elastic ends, stitch the ends to a small piece of fabric side by side. This will eliminate extra bulk within the casing. Avoid difficulties when feeding the elastic through the casing by preparing the seam allowances that are inside. On lightweight fabrics, press them open to one side and feed the elastic in the same direction. On medium- to heavyweight fabrics, press the seam allowances open and attach them to the garment with a bit of hemming tape.

METHOD 1
FOLDED-DOWN CASING

In this method, the casing is created by extending the top of the skirt or trouser fabric piece. (On commercial patterns, the extra fabric needed for a casing will be incorporated in the pattern piece.)

1 To calculate the amount of fabric needed to form the casing when making your own patterns, measure the width of elastic being used and add 6 mm (¼ in.) for seam allowance plus 10 mm (⅜ in.) for ease. So for elastic that is 20 mm (¾ in.) wide, you need to extend the top of the waist of the skirt or trousers by 36 mm (1⅜ in.).

2 Neaten the top edge. On lightweight fabrics, turn the raw edge of the extended waist under by 6 mm (¼ in.) and press. On medium to heavyweight fabrics, neaten the raw edge by overcast stitch or zigzag stitch and press. On fabrics that don't fray, you do not need to neaten the top edge.

3 Turn the neatened top edge under along the waistline and press again.

4 Machine stitch close to the inner fold, leaving a gap of at least 5 cm (2 in.) through which to insert the elastic. Stitch around the casing again, this time 2–3 mm (⅛ in.) from the top edge.

5 Attach the elastic to a bodkin (a needle-like tool with a blunt or bobble end) or a safety pin and then feed it 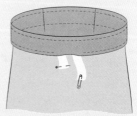 through the casing, making sure the other end of the elastic doesn't disappear within casing by pinning it to the garment at the start of the gap. Ease the waistline fabric along as you feed the elastic through.

6 Bring the elastic back out of the gap and pin the ends securely to a small square of fabric. Try on the garment and check for fit, pulling up more elastic if needed.

7 Machine stitch the elastic ends to the fabric scrap to secure before easing them back into the casing. Re-adjust the gathers evenly. Slipstitch the opening closed.

8 To prevent the elastic from twisting during laundering, stitch vertically down through all 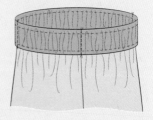 thicknesses at the side seams and at the centre back seam, if applicable. This will also help keep the gathers even.

METHOD 2
APPLIED CASING

The casing is created from another fabric – ideally something lightweight and flexible, such as ribbon, bias binding or a strip of bias-cut fabric. This is the most frequently used method for dresses or jumpsuits. It is also a useful method to use when a self-fabric casing might be too bulky.

1 To calculate the width of the casing fabric or bias binding needed, measure the width of the elastic being used and add 12 mm (½ in.) for seam allowances plus 10 mm (⅜ in.) for ease. So elastic 20 mm (¾ in.) wide, would need casing 42 mm (1⅝ in) wide. The casing should be long enough to go around the garment ungathered, plus 3 cm (1¼ in.) to neaten the ends.

2 Cut the casing strip to the measurement calculated in step 1. Then turn one long edge of the strip to the wrong side by 6 mm (¼ in.) and press.

3 Turn the garment wrong side out. Starting close to a seam, begin pinning the un-neatened long edge of the casing strip right side down to the casing position, turning the short end of the strip over by 1 cm (⅜ in.). Pin and stitch the casing strip all the way around, overlapping the short ends by 2 cm (¾ in.).

4 Press and then flip the casing fabric up. Pin and stitch the top edge of the casing strip to the garment.

5 Calculate the length of elastic needed and insert following steps 5–8 of Method 1.

6 To prevent the elastic from twisting during laundering, stitch vertically down through all thicknesses at the side seams and at centre back seam, if applicable (see step 8 of Method 1). This will also help keep the gathers even.

METHOD 3
QUARTERING THE ELASTIC

With this method you do not create a casing, just attach the elastic to the garment edge. This method is often used in children's wear, sportswear and lingerie.

1 Determine the amount of fabric needed to cover the elastic, once attached, by taking the elastic width and adding a 6 mm (¼ in.) seam allowance. Then neaten the top edge of the garment ready for elastic application.

2 Cut the elastic to the waist measurement less 2.5 cm (1 in.). Overlap the ends by 2.5 cm (1 in.) and machine stitch together to produce a continuous loop of elastic.

3 Divide the elastic loop into four equal quarters and mark with pins. Divide the garment top into four equal quarters, again marking with pins (i.e., centre back/front and side seams).

4 Matching the quarter marks on the garment and the elastic, pin the elastic to the WRONG side of the garment with neatened garment edge and elastic edge together. Using a triple zigzag stitch, anchor the elastic to the garment from first to second quarter mark, pulling the elastic taut to fit between the pins. Continue to stitch the elastic to the garment, stretching the elastic to fit each section.

5 Fold the elastic to the inside of the garment, effectively encasing the elastic at the same time. Keep it in place by stitching through all thicknesses at the side seams and centre back seam, if applicable.

150 CM (60 IN.) WIDE FABRIC

115 CM (45 IN.) WIDE FABRIC

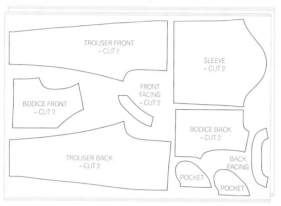

INTERFACING

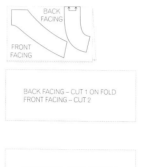

BACK FACING – CUT 1 ON FOLD
FRONT FACING – CUT 2

BACK FACING – CUT 1 ON FOLD
POCKET – CUT 4

LAYOUT PLAN

If your fabric is 115 cm (45 in.) wide, cut it in half across the width, and then turn one piece over and lay it right side down on top of the other – both opened out flat, with the selvedges matching. If your fabric is 150 cm (60 in.) wide, fold it in half widthways. Trace off the pattern pieces – bodice front, bodice back, trouser front, trouser back, sleeve, front facing, back facing, pocket. After preparing your fabric, fold it as shown on the layout for the width of fabric you are working with. Lay out the pattern pieces as shown. Measure to the selvedge to make sure that the grain is straight. Cut out and transfer any markings to the fabric (see Get Set to Sew, page 21).

1 Staystitch (see page 29) the bodice front and back neck edges 13 mm (½ in.) from the edge by stitching with a regular 2.5 stitch length just inside the seam allowance, sewing from the side edges to the centre.

2 STITCH THE DARTS
Following the instructions on page 150, fold, pin and stitch the waist darts in the bodice back and the bust and waist darts in the bodice front pieces. Press the waist darts towards the centre front or back, and the bust darts downwards.

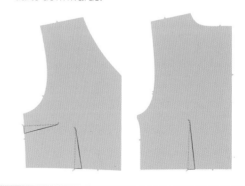

3 With right sides together, pin and stitch the back bodice pieces together. Neaten the seam allowances and press the seam open. With right sides together, matching the notches, pin and stitch the bodice fronts to the back at the shoulders and side seams. Neaten the seam allowances and press the seams open.

4 Following the instructions on page 150, fold, pin and stitch the darts in the trouser backs and fronts. Press the waist darts towards the centre back.

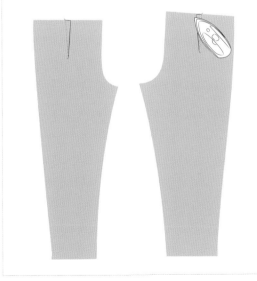

5 ATTACH THE POCKETS
With right sides together, matching the notches and aligning the raw edges, pin one pocket to a trouser front. Stitch, taking a 1-cm (⅜-in.) seam. Press the seam towards the pocket. Apply the remaining pocket pieces to the other trouser front and the trouser back pieces in the same way.

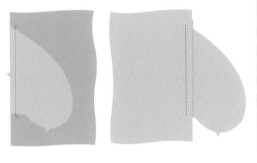

6 MAKE THE JUMPSUIT
With right sides together, pin one trouser front to one trouser back at the inside leg and stitch. Repeat for the other trouser leg. Neaten the seam allowances and press the seams towards the back.

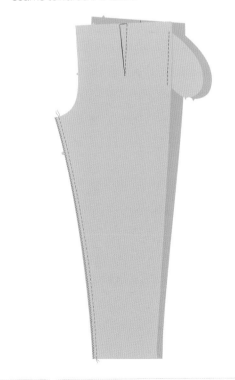

CORE SKILL
Exposed and surface-mounted zip insertions

Attaching a zip has traditionally been done to conceal the zip teeth and make the opening as discreet as possible. Now, with the introduction of prettier zips and new construction methods, zips can mounted in full, glorious view as a design detail.

EXPOSED ZIP

This method just has the teeth on view, with no stitching visible on the right side of the garment.

1 Neaten the raw edges of the seam allowances into which the zip is to be inserted. Press. Fuse strips of interfacing 2.5 cm (1 in.) wide to the wrong side of the zip placement area on each piece.

2 On the wrong side of the fabric, mark the zip placement lines with a chalk pencil, marking the length to just below the zip stop and the sides 2 cm (¾ in.) 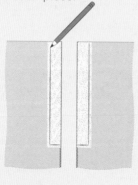 either side of the neatened edges. Hand or machine tack along the marked lines.

3 Snip diagonally into the seam allowances, starting 1 cm (⅜ in.) above the end of the basting and down towards the corners, making sure you don't clip the basting stitching.

4 Fold the seam allowance of the zip placement areas to the wrong side along the tacking stitching and press.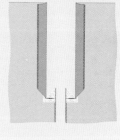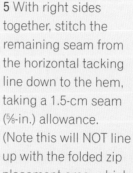

5 With right sides together, stitch the remaining seam from the horizontal tacking line down to the hem, taking a 1.5-cm seam (⅝-in.) allowance. (Note this will NOT line up with the folded zip placement area, which has been folded at 2 cm/¾ in.).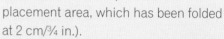

6 Press the seam allowances open. Note that, above the seam, the zip opening has a gap and the little triangles of fabric are pointing up.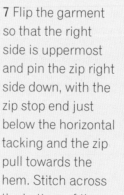

7 Flip the garment so that the right side is uppermost and pin the zip right side down, with the zip stop end just below the horizontal tacking and the zip pull towards the hem. Stitch across the bottom of the zip, in line with the previous tacking – just across the centre of the zip, not all the way across the zip tape.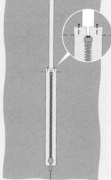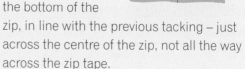

8 Flip the zip up and push it to the inside of the garment, so that only the teeth are exposed from the right side. On the wrong side, the little triangles of fabric should now be pointing downwards.

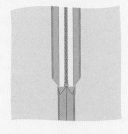

9 Turn the garment right side out and anchor the zip tape to the seam allowance only, using double-sided tape or temporary glue. Turn back one side so that only the seam allowance is uppermost, with the zip tape in place underneath. Machine sew down the vertical tacking stitches. Repeat for the other side of the zip.

10 Turn the garment over and you will see a beautifully inserted zip with the teeth exposed.

SURFACE-MOUNTED ZIP

In this method, the whole zip is attached to the right side of the garment – a perfect use for the pretty lacy-edged zip tapes now available.

1 Prepare the seam allowances, following steps 1 and 2 of the Exposed Zip, opposite.

2 Place the fabric pieces right sides together and, taking a regular 1.5-cm (⅝-in.) seam allowance, stitch the seam below the zip opening.

3 As before, clip diagonally into the seam allowances at the base of the zip placement area. Then press the triangles formed at

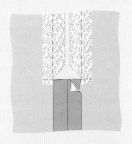

the zip base to the wrong side under the seam allowance. Press the seam allowance open below the zip opening.

4 For the zip opening, turn the seam allowance to the right side along the machine tacking and press.

5 On the right side of the fabric, place the zip right side down, with the zip stop end just below the horizontal tacking and the zip pull towards the hem. Stitch across the bottom of the zip tape, just below the zip stop (see Exposed Zip, step 7).

6 Flip the zip up over the exposed seam allowances (the teeth will be over the gap between the two fabric pieces and some seam allowance will

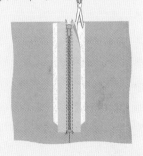

extend beyond the zip tape on either side). Attach a zipper foot to your machine. Pin, tack and machine stitch the zip tape to the seam allowance, close to the teeth.

7 Carefully trim back the seam allowance from under the zip tape, taking care not to cut the zip tape or the garment fabric beneath.

8 Again with the zipper foot attached, stitch the zip tape again down the outer edges, effectively encasing the raw edge of the zip opening under the zip tape.

7 With right sides together, stitch one trouser front to a trouser back at the side seams, pivoting at the large circle at the top of the pocket, stitching around the pocket and pivoting again at the bottom large circle before continuing down the side seam. Clip diagonally into the seam allowance below the pocket. Repeat for the other trouser leg. Press the seams towards the back.

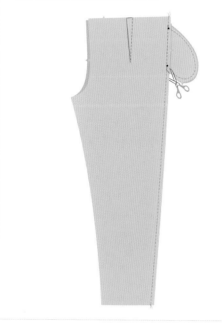

9 To stitch the crotch seam, turn one trouser leg right side out and slip it into the other one so that the right sides are together, matching the side and centre seams. Stitch from the centre back to the large circle. Stitch again close to the first row, just within the seam allowance, then trim the seam allowance close to the stitching. Press the seam open. Turn the trousers right side out.

8 Turn the pockets towards the front pieces along the seam lines. Press and tack the pockets to the upper edge.

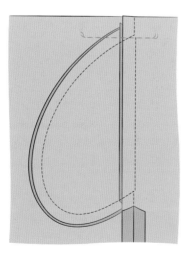

10 With right sides together, matching the seams, darts and raw edges, pin the bodice over the waistline of the trousers. Stitch, then press the seam allowances up towards the bodice.

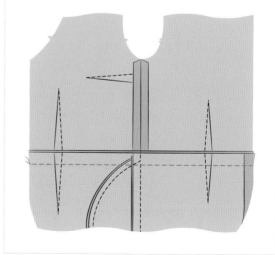

11 MAKE THE WAISTLINE SIDE CASINGS

To form the waistline casing for the side elastic, cut two 15-cm (6-in.) lengths of bias binding. Open out one long edge of the bias binding and fold the short end in by 6 mm (¼ in.). Pin the binding to the seam allowance on the inside of the garment between the dots at the sides, placing the crease from the fold of the binding close to the seam between the bodice and the trousers. At the other end of the binding, again turn the short end of the bias tape in. Stitch in the crease. Repeat for the other side seam.

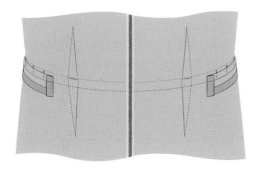

12

Press the binding up towards the bodice and stitch along the top edge through all thicknesses.

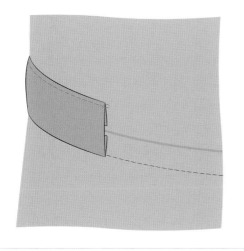

13

Fuse 2.5-cm (1-in.) strips of interfacing to the wrong side of the zip-placement area on the centre front bodices. Insert an exposed zip, following the instructions on page 62. (With this method, the teeth of the zip are exposed as a design feature, but no stitching is visible on the right side of the garment.).

14 ATTACH THE FACINGS

Apply the interfacing pieces to the front facing and back fabric facings. With right sides together, stitch the facing sections together at the shoulder seams. Then neaten the outer edge of the facing by overlocking, overedge stitching or turning a narrow hem (see page 43).

15

With right sides together, matching the notches and shoulder seams, pin the facing to the bodice. Stitch the neck edge. Grade the seam allowance by cutting the garment seam allowance nearest the garment to 1 cm (⅜ in.) and the facing seam allowance to 6 mm (¼ in.).

TIP

If you are using medium-weight interfacing, first trim 1 cm (⅜ in.) all the way around the edges, then centre the interfacing on the facing pieces and fuse in place.

16

Understitch (see page 29) the facing along the neck edge. Turn the facing to the inside of the garment. Slipstitch (see page 31) the edge of the facing to the zip tape and the facing to the shoulder seams.

17 Ease stitch (stitch two rows just inside seam line with a long stitch length) the upper edge of the sleeve between the notches. With right sides together, matching the notches, fold and stitch the sleeve. Repeat for the second sleeve.

18 Neaten the raw edge of the sleeve by overlocking, overedge or zigzag stitching. Turn up 2.5 cm (1 in.) and slipstitch in place. Press.

19 With right sides together, pin the sleeve into the armhole, placing the large circle at the shoulder seam. Adjust the ease, tack and stitch. Stitch again. Trim and neaten the raw edges together. Press the seam towards the sleeve. Repeat for the second sleeve.

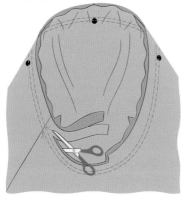

20 Cut two pieces of elastic 5 cm (2 in.) longer than the bias binding. Attach the safety pin to one end of the elastic and feed it through the binding from one side around and out the other, making sure that the free end doesn't disappear inside the casing. Pin the elastic through all layers to anchor the start and end of the elastic to hold it in place while you try on the jumpsuit. Check for comfort and adjust the elastic if necessary by pulling up more of the elastic to tighten or allowing a little extra. Once you are happy with the fit, stitch vertically down through the casing and the elastic to anchor it in place.

21 Turn the lower edge of the legs to the wrong side by 3 cm (1¼ in.) and press. Press under the raw edge by 6 mm (¼ in.) and stitch close to the inner edge to finish the hem.

22 MAKE A BELT (OPTIONAL)

Cut two pieces of fabric measuring 94 x 13 cm (37 x 5 in.) and stitch them together at one short end. With right sides together, fold the belt in half widthways. Stitch the short ends and the long unfolded edge, leaving a 20-cm (8-in.) opening in the centre of the long edge. Trim the seam allowance and cut off the corners at an angle.

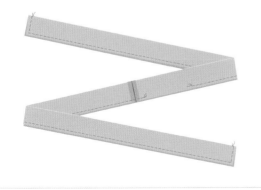

23

Turn the belt right side out and press. Slipstitch the opening closed.

DESIGNER TIPS

- You can adapt this design to make the bodice in one fabric and the trousers in another to look like a top and trousers. Use a slinky silky fabric for the top and a gabardine for the trousers.

- Change the zip for a regular lapped (see page 122 or concealed zip (see page 108) in the front.

BABYGROW

BABYGROW

Cotton stretch fabric, like cotton jersey, is perfect for babies and toddlers as it moves with them, is breathable, feels comfortable next to the skin and is washable. This is a great project if you'd like to practise working with stretch fabric and binding edges with patterned jersey.

MATERIALS
2.3 m (2½ yd) cotton jersey fabric, 115 cm (45 in.) wide, with a minimum of 30% stretch

6–9 jersey snap fasteners

Matching sewing thread

Snap fastener pliers (optional)

Ballpoint sewing machine needle

Basic sewing kit (see page 10)

DIFFICULTY LEVEL
Intermediate

FABRIC SUGGESTIONS
Cotton jersey.

DESIGN NOTES
This babygrow has snap fasteners attached with special pliers, but you can also use the same snap fasteners and apply with the tool provided and a hammer. Apart from attaching the binding, the babygrow shown here was made on an overlocker, but you could make it on a sewing machine instead, using a ballpoint needle and zigzag or stretch stitch.

Use a 1-cm (⅜-in.) seam allowance throughout, unless otherwise stated.

Check the stretch of your fabric for this project: a 5-cm (2 -in.) square should stretch from the grey to white area.

5CM OF FABRIC SHOULD STRETCH FROM HERE TO AT LEAST HERE →

AGE in months	9	12	18	24	30	36
CHEST (cm)	47.5	49	50.25	51.75	53	54.5
CHEST (in.)	18⅝	19¼	19¾	20⅜	20⅞	21½
WAIST (cm)	48	49.5	80.75	52.25	53.5	55
WAIST (in.)	18⅞	19½	20	20½	21 1/16	21⅝

CORE SKILL
Embellishing with appliqué

Appliqué is a technique involving sewing a small piece of fabric onto a larger one to create a design. An appliqué is a motif or shape used to embellish a garment. You can buy ready-made appliqués or create your own from small pieces of fabric.

TIPS

- Choose an appliqué fabric with the same laundering needs as the main garment.

- Back the area on which the appliqué is to be sewn with stabiliser or interfacing to give added support.

- Most fabric appliqués are sewn with a satin stitch, which neatly covers the raw edges of the appliqué, preventing  it from fraying. Alternative stitches include blanket stitch, with the straight part around the edge of the appliqué and the little horizontal part going into the appliqué. If the appliqué fabric doesn't fray, you can use a straight stitch around the edge.

HOW TO APPLIQUÉ

1 Decide on the appliqué shape. Select an appropriate fabric for the appliqué and fuse a paper-backed double-sided fusible web to  the wrong side. Draw around a shape or draw your own on the paper backing. Once it is cool, neatly cut around the shape.

2 Peel away the paper backing and then place the design on the garment in the desired position. Cover with a press cloth and fuse in  place with a hot iron. This will hold the appliqué in position while you stitch. If the appliqué is to be a combination of fabrics, such as a flower with a centre and leaves, repeat step 1 for each element, fusing them in place on the garment.

3 Attach a satin stitch foot to your machine and select a stitch to sew around the appliqué. If using a satin stitch, select the zigzag stitch and reduce the length to 0.35–0.4 and reduce the width to 3. Test the result on a sample of fabric.

4 Back the main fabric under the appliqué area with interfacing or a stabiliser – either a soluble variety that can be washed away later or a tear-away version that is torn away once stitching is complete.

5 Sew around the design so the right swing of the needle stitches into the garment and the left swing of the needle sews into  the appliqué. To ensure you stitch smoothly around curves, at outward curves, stop with the needle down in the garment, raise the presser foot, turn the fabric slightly, lower the presser foot and continue. For inner curves, stop with needle in the appliqué fabric, raise the presser foot, pivot and continue.

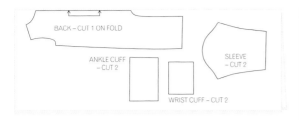

BACK – CUT 1 ON FOLD

ANKLE CUFF – CUT 2

WRIST CUFF – CUT 2

SLEEVE – CUT 2

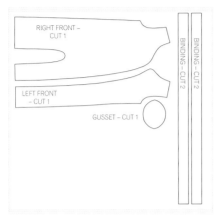

RIGHT FRONT – CUT 1

LEFT FRONT – CUT 1

GUSSET – CUT 1

BINDING – CUT 2

BINDING – CUT 2

LAYOUT PLAN

Trace off the pattern pieces – right front, left front, back, ankle cuff, wrist cuff, gusset, binding and sleeve. After preparing your fabric, fold it as shown on the layout. Lay out the pattern pieces as shown, cutting the front pieces as a single layer, with both fabric and pattern right side up so that the pieces don't 'mirror' onto the wrong half of the body. Measure to the selvedge to make sure that the grain is straight. Cut out and transfer any markings to the fabric (see Get Set to Sew, page 21).

1 STITCH THE SHOULDER SEAMS

Lay out the back piece, right side up. Position the left front piece (the narrower front piece) on top of the back piece, right sides together, aligning the raw edges at the shoulders. Pin together. Position the right front piece (the wider front piece) on top of the back piece in the same way and pin together. Stitch the fronts and the back together at the shoulder seams. Press the seams towards the front.

2 ATTACH THE BINDING

Place the binding pieces right sides together, aligning the raw edges at one short end. Pin and stitch together. Press the seam open. Finish one of the long raw edges, using an overlocker-style stitch if you're making this on a regular sewing machine.

3 With right sides together, matching the centre back seam of the binding to the centre back notch of the babygrow, pin the raw long edge of the binding around the neckline, gently easing the pieces together round the curve by slightly stretching the binding as necessary. When you reach the corners at the front of the neckline, continue to align the raw edges and pin the binding to the curved edges carefully without stretching either. Pin the remaining lengths of the binding to the front edges of the babygrow. Note the binding will be a little longer than the left front edge (the narrower front piece). Trim away the excess so that the binding is the same length as the front piece on this side.

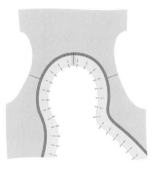

4 If you are using an overlocker, then you need to switch to a sewing machine to attach the binding. Using a 1.5-cm (⅝-in.) seam allowance and a straight stitch on your machine, sew the binding to the front edges and neckline in one continuous seam, from bottom left to bottom right. At both ends of this seam, trim away 2 cm (¾ in.) of the seam allowance approximately 2 mm (a scant ⅛ in.) away from the stitching line. This will reduce the bulk when you attach the ankle cuffs.

5 Press both the seam allowance and the binding away from the babygrow. Lay out the babygrow, wrong side up. Press the binding over the seam allowance so that the finished edge of the binding just covers the seam line.

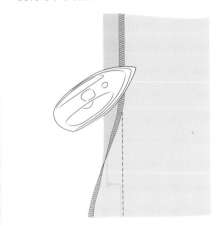

6 With the babygrow right side up, pin the binding in place as you have pressed it. Topstitch through the binding approximately 2–3mm (⅛ in.) away from the seam line, with a stitch length of 3. Press the binding.

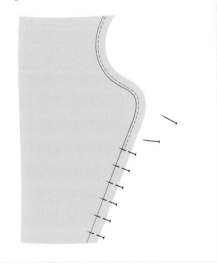

7 Place the babygrow right side up, with the binding at the right front piece (the wider front piece) sitting on top of the binding at the left front piece (the narrower front piece). Keeping the back legs out of the way, pin the fronts together. Machine baste the raw binding ends together where you have pinned, 5 mm (about ¼ in.) from the edge of the ankle. Topstitch across the binding through all the layers, 2 cm (¾ in.) away from the row of basting stitching.

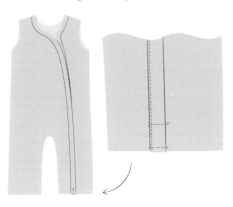

8 ATTACH THE SLEEVES
Lay out the babygrow right side up, so that the armholes form smooth curves. Ascertain which is the correct sleeve for each armhole curve by checking the notches (matching singles to singles and doubles to doubles). With right sides together, matching the central sleeve head notch with the shoulder seam, position one of the sleeves on top of the corresponding armhole curve. Pin together. Next, match the single notch on the sleeve head with the single notch on the armhole curve and pin together. Do the same with the double notches. Finally, match the underarm points of the sleeve with the beginning and end points of the armhole curve and pin.

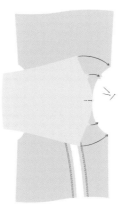

TIP

In steps 8, 11 and 12, because you are joining a convex curve to a concave curve, you will need to gently ease the edges together and you may wish to add more pins in between the matched points.

9 Switch back to the overlocker at this point, if you are using one. Stitch the sleeve head to the armhole curve, making sure the shoulder seam remains laying in the direction that you previously pressed it. Repeat steps 8 and 9 for the remaining sleeve.

10 STITCH THE SIDE SEAMS
With the front and back pieces right sides together, matching the underarm seams and the notches on the sides, pin together. Stitch the sleeves and sides of the front and back pieces together.

11 ATTACH THE GUSSET

Lay out the babygrow right side out, with the front facing up. With right sides together, matching the centre front notches, position the gusset on top of the inside leg and pin at this point. Match the gusset side notches with the corresponding notches at the front inside leg and pin together at these points. Stitch the gusset to the front inside leg.

12

Turn the babygrow wrong side out and lay it out with the back facing up. With right sides together, matching the centre back notches, position the gusset underneath the back inside leg and pin at this point. Match the gusset side notches with the corresponding notches at the back inside leg and pin together at these points. Matching the lower inside leg notches, pin the front and back inside legs together. Stitch the inside legs together, including the remaining half of the gusset. Check that there are no holes at the sides of the gusset.

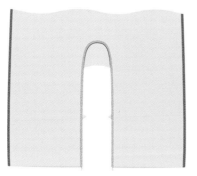

13 ATTACH THE WRIST AND ANKLE CUFFS

Fold one cuff piece in half widthways, right sides together, matching the notches. Pin and stitch together into a circle. Turn right side out, then fold so that the raw edges are aligned. Press lightly along the folded edge. Repeat for the three remaining cuff pieces.

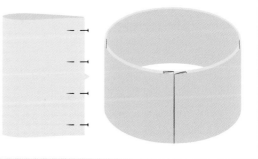

14

Flatten an ankle cuff so that the seamline becomes a fold. Mark the opposite fold at the raw edge with a pin. Turn the babygrow right side out. Aligning the raw edges and matching the cuff seam with the inside leg seam and the pin on the cuff with the side seam of the babygrow, slip the ankle cuff over one leg. Pin together. Note that the cuff will be slightly smaller than the babygrow leg, so ease them together by stretching the cuff slightly as you pin. Stitch the cuff to the bottom of the babygrow leg.

15 Repeat step 14 for the remaining ankle cuff, and attach the two wrist cuffs to the sleeves in the same way. Before slipping the wrist cuffs over the sleeves, mark the point opposite the sleeve seam (which will appear as a fold if the babygrow is lying flat) on the raw edge with a pin.

16 Using tailor's chalk or a fabric marker pen, mark the position of the fastenings on the centre front bindings, spacing them evenly. Attach press studs, snaps or poppers at these points, following the instructions for attaching snaps that come with the packet (or see page 166).

CHILD'S

CAPE

CHILD'S CAPE

A cape is easy to wear and comfortable. This one is made from a lovely wool and lined with cotton. You can as easily make it in satin and leave it unlined as a costume cape for dressing up.

MATERIALS
2.3 m (2½ yd) fabric 115 cm (45 in.) wide, or 1.6 m (1¾ yd) fabric 150 cm (60 in.) wide

2.3 m (2½ yd) lining fabric 115 cm (45 in.) wide, or 1.6 m (1¾ yd) lining fabric 150 cm (60 in.) wide

1 frog fastening

Matching machine thread

Basic sewing kit (see page 10)

DIFFICULTY LEVEL
Beginner

FABRIC SUGGESTIONS
Lightweight wool, wool mixtures, satin or velvet.

DESIGN NOTES
This cape could be made without the hood or with a collar. It could also be made longer to go over a special-occasion outfit.

Use a 1.5-cm (⅝-in.) seam allowance throughout.

AGE in years	4	5	6	7	8	9
WAIST (cm)	132.75	134.75	137.25	139.75	141.75	145
WAIST (in.)	52¼	53	54	55	55¾	57 ¹⁄₁₆
LENGTH (cm)	48.5	50.5	52.5	54.5	56.5	58.5
LENGTH (in.)	19⅛	19⅞	20⅝	21½	22¼	23
WIDTH AT HEM (cm)	204.25	206.25	208.75	211.25	213.25	216.5
WIDTH AT HEM (in.)	80⅜	81¼	82⅛	83⅛	84	85¼

CORE SKILL
Sewing with slippery or sticky fabrics

Stitching fabrics that tend to slip or stick because of the coating on the surface can be tricky and frustrating, as they fail to feed properly. But with a few tricks and tips, these problems are solved!

SLIPPERY FABRICS
CUTTING OUT AND PINNING

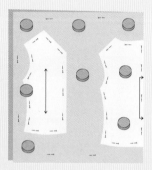

Pin the fabric layers together at the selvedge and ends to prevent them from shifting. Pin frequently, keeping the pins within the seam allowance, using new sharp pins. Placing weights on top will also hold the layers together while you pin patterns to them. Cut out with long strokes, using the full length of the shears.

NEEDLES
Use a fine Universal Sharps needle, size 70/9. Start with a new needle each time, as a blunt needle can snag the fabric and cause skipped stitches.

INTERFACING
Take care the interfacing doesn't swamp the fabric or show through on the right side. For transparent fabrics, use another layer of the fashion fabric as interfacing. For lightweight silks and satins, a woven sew-in interfacing is preferable.

MACHINE SEWING
Use a stitch length of 2.2–2.5 for most seams. Lightweight, fine fabrics can get pulled into the feed dogs at the start of a seam, so to avoid this start seams approximately 1.5 cm (⅝ in.) from the end, holding on to the thread tails, then reverse back to the beginning, before continuing forwards. If the fabric still tends to be pulled down into the feed dogs at the beginning, place a little piece of tissue paper below the fabric and stitch with that in place. Tear it away after you've stitched the seam.

STICKY FABRICS
CUTTING OUT AND PINNING
When working with 'sticky' fabrics such as PVC, oilcloths, some waxed cottons, or faux suede, you may need to cut out and pin with more care than usual, because the fabric layers can stick together. To overcome these problems, cut out from single layers, with the fabric right side up. To cut two of the same pattern piece, cut the first and then flip the pattern over to cut the corresponding second piece to ensure you get a left and a right. Use weights to hold the pattern in place. To hold layers together for seaming, use bulldog clips or paper clips rather than pinning. (Note that pins may leave permanent holes in the cloth – so if you do have to pin, only pin in the seam allowance.)

MACHINE SEWING
If the fabrics are heavyweight, creating bulky seams, increase the stitch length to 2.8–3 for seaming and then grade the seams by cutting one to a scant 6 mm (¼ in.) and the other to 1 cm (⅜ in.). Sew with a walking, roller or Teflon foot to help feed the fabric layers evenly.

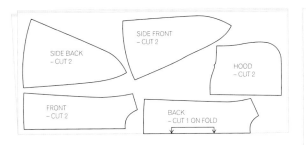

LAYOUT
PLAN

Fold the fabric in half widthways, right sides together, aligning the selvedges. Lay the pattern pieces on the fabric as shown, measuring from the grainline to the selvedge to check that they are straight. Cut one of each piece in your main fabric and one in lining fabric. Transfer any pattern markings to the fabric (see Get Set to Sew, page 21).

3 With right sides together, stitch the back to the side back sections. Press the seams open. Stitch the front to the back at the shoulder seams. Press the seams open.

4 Repeat steps 1–3 to make up the cape lining.

1 ASSEMBLE THE CAPE PIECES
Staystitch the front and back neck edges 13 mm (½ in.) from the edge with a 2.5 stitch length just inside the seam allowance.

5 MAKE THE HOOD
To make the hood, first make the pleats in the lower edge of the hood. With the right side of the hood facing up, fold the first hood piece along the solid line fold along the solid line marked on the pattern, bring the fold to the broken line, then tack across the raw lower edge to hold the pleat in place. Repeat on the other hood piece.

2 With right sides together, pin and stitch the fronts to the side front sections, leaving an opening between the dots for the hand holes. Backstitch at the dots to reinforce the seams and press open, ensuring the unstitched sections are pressed back, too.

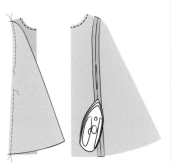

6 Pin the two hood pieces right sides together, matching the notches. Stitch the centre seam, clip the curves (see page 43) and press.

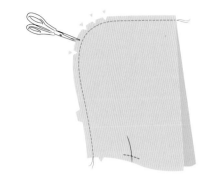

10 Clip into the seam allowance of the neck edge of the cape to the staystitching.

11 **ATTACH THE HOOD TO THE CAPE AND ADD THE LINING**
With right sides together, matching the centre back seams and notches, pin the hood to the neck edge of the cape. Tack in place.

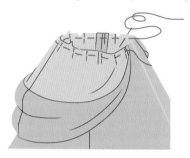

7 Trim away the front edge of the hood lining pieces along the fold line. Repeat steps 5 and 6 to make up the hood lining.

8 With right sides together, matching the seams and aligning the raw edges, place the lining fabric hood over the main fabric hood and pin together. Stitch around the front opening and press the seam towards the lining.

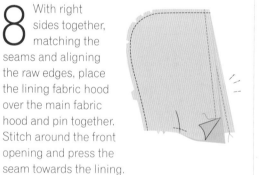

12 With right sides together, matching the centre back seams, side seams and notches, pin the lining to the cape, over the hood. Stitch around the neck, front and lower edge. Grade the seam allowances (see page 43) by cutting one side to 6 mm (¼ in.) and the other to 1 cm (⅜ in.).

9 Turn the hood right side out and press. Matching the seams and notches, tack the main and lining fabric hoods together along the raw bottom edge.

13 Turn the cape right side out through one side front opening. Press.

15 Hand stitch a frog fastener to the top of the front of the cape.

14 At the side front openings, slipstitch (see page 31) the pressed-back edges of the lining and outer cape hand holes together.

UNISEX KIMONO

UNISEX KIMONO

Kimonos have been worn as loungewear by men, women and children for a long time, as well as being a fashionable garment. Easy to make and easy to wear, this is an ideal project for matching his'n'hers presents.

MATERIALS
3.9–4.2 m (4¼–4½ yd) cotton or silky polyester 115 cm (45 in.) wide, or 3.2–3.7 m (3½–4 yd) cotton or silky polyester 150 cm (60 in.) wide

2.1 m (2¼ yd) co-ordinating cotton or silk, 115 or 150 cm (45 or 60 in.) wide, for the contrast bands

1.5 m (1⅝ yd) iron-on interfacing

Matching sewing thread

Basic sewing kit (see page 10)

DIFFICULTY LEVEL
Beginner

FABRIC SUGGESTIONS
While silky fabric is the material that most people associate with kimonos, a lightweight cotton is a great alternative for loungewear. You can also use this pattern to make snuggly dressing gowns in fleece. Cut all pieces on the lengthwise grain (see page 20), regardless of your fabric choice.

DESIGN NOTES
Kimonos are cut from basic rectangles – a simple shape that provides an ideal showcase for beautiful fabrics. Kimonos are easy to sew because they are constructed using straight seams. Neatening the raw edges of all pieces before you stitch them together will save time.

Use a 1-cm (⅜-in.) seam allowance throughout.

FINISHED MEASUREMENTS	36	38	40	42	44	46	48
CHEST (cm)	118.5	120	121.25	122.5	123.75	125	126.25
CHEST (in.)	46¾	47¼	47¾	48¼	48¾	49¼	49¾
WAIST (cm)	116	117.25	118.5	119.75	121	122.25	123.5
WAIST (in.)	45⅝	46⅛	46⅝	47⅛	47⅝	48⅛	48⅝
WIDTH AT HEM (cm)	133	134.25	135.5	136.75	138	139.25	140.5
WIDTH AT HEM (in.)	52⅜	52⅞	53⅜	53⅞	54⅜	54⅞	55⅜

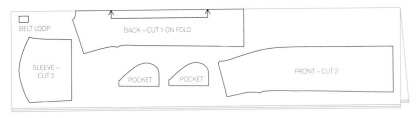

BELT LOOP

BACK – CUT 1 ON FOLD

SLEEVE – CUT 2

POCKET   POCKET

FRONT – CUT 2

SLEEVE BAND

BELT – CUT 2

FRONT CONTRAST BAND

SLEEVE BAND – CUT 2
FRONT CONTRAST BANDS –
CUT 2 IN MAIN FABRIC AND 2 IN INTERFACING
POCKET – CUT 4
BELT LOOP – CUT 2

LAYOUT PLAN

Trace off the pattern pieces – back, front, sleeve, sleeve band, contrast band, pocket, belt and belt loops. After preparing your fabric, fold it as shown on the layout for the width of fabric you are working with. Lay out the pattern pieces as shown. Measure to the selvedge to make sure that the grain is straight. Cut out and transfer any markings to the fabric (see Get Set to Sew, page 21).

1 MAKE THE KIMONO
Neaten the edges of all pieces all the way around (see page 41). Staystitch the neck edge of the kimono back by stitching with a regular 2.5 stitch length just inside the seam allowance, sewing from the side edges to the centre.

2 With right sides together, pin and then sew the back piece to the front pieces at the shoulder seams. Press the seams open.

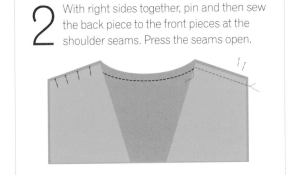

3 Open out the garment. With right sides together, matching the notches and matching the small centre dot on the sleeve to the shoulder seam, pin the sleeve to the armhole edge. Sew, then press the seam towards the sleeve.

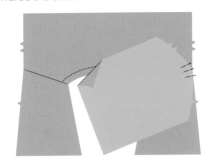

4 With right sides together, stitch the straight edge of one pocket piece to each garment front at the marked position. Now attach the remaining two pocket pieces to the kimono back, matching the placement lines.

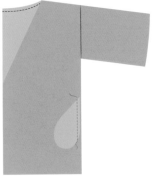

5 Press all seams towards the pockets, then press the pockets away from the garment.

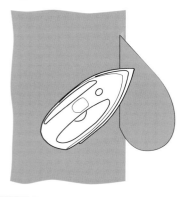

6 With right sides together, pin the front of the kimono to the back at the side and underarm seams, matching the front and back of the sleeves. Pin around the pocket pieces. On each side, stitch from the sleeve edge towards the underarm, then pivot with the needle in the fabric and stitch down to the top of the pocket. Pivot again and stitch around the pocket pieces, then pivot again to stitch the remaining garment seam. Reinforce the underarm and pocket top and bottom by stitching again for 5 cm (2 in.) either side of the pivot points. Clip into the seam allowance where the pocket joins the garment at the lower edge and press the pocket towards the garment front.

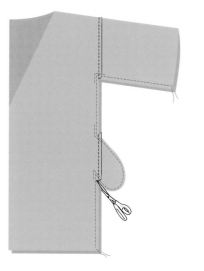

7 ATTACH THE CONTRAST BANDS
Cut interfacing to half the width of the contrast band pieces and fuse it to the wrong side of the bands down one long edge (so that the inner edge of the interfacing is along the fold line of the band). Allow to cool. With right sides together, stitch the band pieces together to create one long strip. Turn the non-interfaced long edge to the wrong side by 1.5 cm (⅝ in.) and press it in place.

8 With right sides together, pin the interfaced long edge of the contrast band to the garment edge. If necessary, clip into the seam allowance of the garment back to help fit the band. Sew from the centre back neck to the lower edge. Repeat for the other side. Press the seams towards the contrast band.

CORE SKILL
Fabric ties and rouleau loops

Fabric ties or fabric belts are used on so many garments and are often made from the same fabric as the garment. Created from strips of fabric cut on the straight grain, they are stitched with straight stitch. Rouleau loops, straps and bag handles are similar, just created from a different size of strip and cut on the bias.   .

Most patterns that require a fabric tie will provide a pattern piece for it. If you are creating your own, determine the length required – remember that it needs to be enough to tie into a bow with tails. Add 3 cm (1¼ in.) to this measurement for the seam allowances. Decide on the width of the finished belt – for a dress or kimono, this may be 3–5 cm (1¼–2 in.). Double this width and add 3 cm (1¼ in.) for the seam allowances.

If you want the belt to have some firmness, interface half the width, applying the interfacing to the wrong side. Use a point turner to turn out the corners neatly.

For very long ties (such as for dressing gowns or tie belts), save on the length of fabric required by dividing the length in half and cutting two pieces side by side. These can then be joined to create one long piece, with the seam at the centre back

SEWING A FABRIC TIE
METHOD 1
This is the standard method for tie belts, and has the seam along the bottom edge and the fold at the top edge.

1 Interface half the tie fabric if required. Once cooled, fold the tie fabric in half lengthways, right sides together, with the raw edges together. Starting at one short

end and taking a 1.5-cm (⅝-in.) seam allowance, stitch across the end, pivot, and stitch along the long edge, leaving a turning gap of about 20 cm (8 in.) in the middle, then continue to the other end, pivoting to stitch the other short end. Trim the seam allowance, leaving the turning gap seam allowance untrimmed. Cut the corners off at an angle, close to the stitching.

2 Turn the tie right side out, pushing the stitched ends through to the opening in the centre with a ruler or other blunt tool. Once turned through, use a point turner to ease out the corners completely.

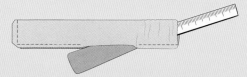

3 Slipstitch the turning gap closed. Press, with the seam on the lower edge of the tie.

SEWING A FABRIC TIE
METHOD 2
Use this method to conceal the seam at the centre back of the tie.

1 Fold the tie fabric in half lengthways, right sides together, with the raw edges together. Stitch along the long edge. Tack across one short end temporarily.

2 Turn the tie through to the right side from the tacked end, pushing the end through with a ruler as in step 2 of Method 1.

3 Unpick the tacking stitches and roll the tube so that the seam runs along the centre. Tuck the seam allowance in at each short end and either edge stitch by machine or slipstitch the opening closed.

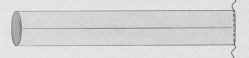

SEWING A FABRIC TIE
METHOD 3
This is a very quick method of making straps and ties, and is particularly useful for fabrics that are thick, sticky or difficult to turn through. The extra rows of stitching also help provide a sturdy tie.

1 With the wrong side uppermost, fold one long edge of the tie to the wrong side by 1 cm (⅜ in.) and press. Fold the other long edge to the centre of the tie and press. Fold the neatened edge to the centre, overlapping the raw edge of the other side. Stitch down the centre close to the fold. Stitch again down either long edge an equal distance from the centre stitching and edges.

2 Turn under the raw ends and edge stitch by machine.

ROULEAU LOOPS
These are narrow ties used as straps on lingerie, to create button loops or as inner ties on a dressing gown. Because they are made from very narrow strips of fabric they can be tricky to turn through, but there are two methods that make it easier.

METHOD 1 – SHOELACE
1 Cut the fabric strip to the width required by the pattern. Fold the fabric in half, right sides together, and then insert a shoelace or length of string that is at least 5 cm (2 in.) longer than the strip into the folded fabric. At one end, centre the lace so that you can tack it in place more easily. Tack across the end to temporarily anchor the shoelace. Then stitch the long edge, keeping the lace out of the way, backstitching at the start and finish.

2 Trim the seam allowance and pull on the shoelace to pull the fabric through to the right side.
You may have to start off the basted end by pushing it inside by hand first.

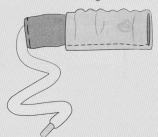

3 Remove the tacking stitches at the end of the tie and take out the shoelace.

METHOD 2 – ROULEAU LOOP TURNER
A rouleau loop turner is a long metal rod with a loop and tiny latched hook at one end. Having stitched the long edges of the tie together, insert the loop turner right to the other end of the tie and hook a little of the fabric onto the hook. Help start turning it through at that end, and then pull on the Loop Turner to bring the fabric through to the right side.

9 To hem the lower edge of the band, fold it in half down the centre, right sides together, and pin the lower edges together. Stitch across the band only, 5 cm (2 in.) up from the ends, from the seam towards the fold. Turn the band right side out. This will effectively turn up the garment hem allowance. The turned-under long edge of the band will now just overlap the seam attaching the band to the garment.

10 Press up the garment hem by 5 cm (2 in.), then turn the edge under again by 2.5 cm (1 in.) so that the raw edge meets the fold. Topstitch it in place.

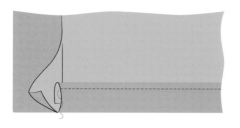

11 Slipstitch (see page 31) the neatened band edge over the seam.

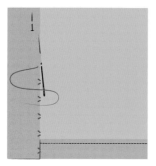

12 ATTACH THE SLEEVE BANDS
Cut the interfacing to half the width of the sleeve bands and fuse it to the wrong side of the bands down one long edge (so that the inner edge of the interfacing is along the fold line of the band). Allow to cool. With right sides together, stitch the short ends of the band together to form a circle. Turn the non-interfaced edge to the wrong side by 1.5 cm (⅝ in.) and press. Attach the band to the sleeve as in step 8, above. Fold the band to the inside, so that the turned-under edge just overlaps the seam attaching the band to the sleeve, and slipstitch it in place.

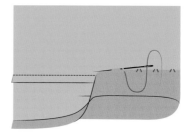

13 MAKE THE BELT AND BELT LOOPS
Pin the belt pieces right sides together and stitch together across one short end to make one long strip. Fold the strip in half lengthways, right sides together. Starting at one short end, stitch across the end, pivot, and stitch along the long edge, leaving a turning gap of at least 15 cm (6 in.) in the middle, then continue to the other end, pivoting to stitch the other short end. Turn the belt right side out and press. Slipstitch the opening closed sleeve, and slipstitch it in place.

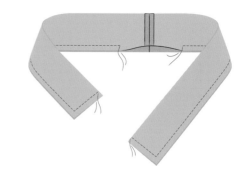

14 Fold the belt loop strips in half lengthways, with right sides together, and stitch along the long edge. Turn right side out, tucking the raw ends inside. Slipstitch closed.

15 Try on the kimono and pin mark the position for the belt loops at the side seams. Hand or machine stitch the ends to the garment at the side seams.

CHAPTER TWO

INSPIRATION

Be inspired. This chapter further develops your sewing skills through projects that take their influences from different cultures and eras. Make your own Chinese-inspired top, as seen on *The Great British Sewing Bee* show, turn a fabulous Indian sari into a dress, or sew your own African-inspired peplum dress in printed waxed cotton. If you love vintage, try the 1960s colour-blocked dress, or the classic palazzo pants and Breton top with a 1930s feel.

BRETON TOP

BRETON TOP

The Breton top is a perennial fashion item that transcends time and trends. Originally known as 'La Mariniere', this traditional cream with navy stripe top was naval uniform for the seamen of Brittany. By including the Breton in her 1917 nautical collection, Coco Chanel popularised the look with both men and women. Permeating across the decades, the classic Breton remains an essential piece in all wardrobes.

MATERIALS
1.5 m (1⅝ yd) fabric, 150 cm (60 in.) wide

25 cm (10 in.) cotton stay tape, 6 mm (¼ in.) wide

Matching sewing thread

Ballpoint needle

Basic sewing kit (see page 10)

DIFFICULTY LEVEL
Beginner

FABRIC SUGGESTIONS
Cotton or viscose jersey.

DESIGN NOTES
This design is a very simple T-shirt with long, straight sleeves and a round neckline. Because it has been stitched in a stretch jersey, there is no need for any additional opening or fastening.

Use a 1.5-cm (⅝-in.) seam allowance throughout.

FINISHED MEASUREMENTS	8	10	12	14	16	18	20
BUST (cm)	107	112	117	122	128	134	140
BUST (in.)	42⅛	44⅛	46¹⁄₁₆	48	50⅜	52¾	55⅛
WAIST (cm)	79.5	84.5	89.5	94.5	100.5	106.5	112.5
WAIST (in.)	31¼	33¼	35¼	37¼	39½	41⅞	44¼

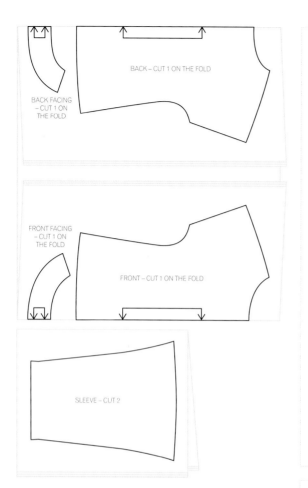

BACK – CUT 1 ON THE FOLD

BACK FACING – CUT 1 ON THE FOLD

FRONT FACING – CUT 1 ON THE FOLD

FRONT – CUT 1 ON THE FOLD

SLEEVE – CUT 2

LAYOUT PLAN

Trace off the pattern pieces – front, back, sleeve, front and back facings. After preparing your fabric, fold the selvedges to the centre, right sides together, and lay out the pattern pieces as shown. Measure to the selvedge to make sure that the grain is straight. Cut out and transfer any markings to the fabric (see Get Set to Sew, page 21). Take care when matching up stripes by cutting each pattern separately, matching notches to stripes.

1 To prevent the shoulder seams from stretching, stay the edges using the cotton tape. Cut the cotton stay tape in half. On the wrong side of the back piece, centre the tape pieces between the neck edge and the notch, 1.5 cm (⅝ in.) from the edge. Tack in place. Staystitch the front and back neck edges 13 mm (½ in.) from the raw edge by stitching with a regular 2.5 stitch length just inside the seam allowance, sewing from the side edges to the centre.

2 With right sides together, stitch the front to the back at the shoulders. Press the seams towards the back.

3 With right sides together, stitch the front and back facings together at the shoulder seams. Press the seams open.

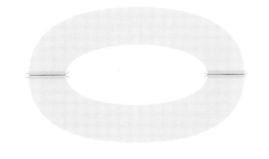

4 With right sides together, matching the shoulder seams, pin the facing to the neck edge and stitch. Grade the seam allowance by cutting the garment side of the seam allowance to 1 cm (⅜ in.) and the facing seam allowance to 6 mm (¼ in.).

5 Press the seam allowance towards the facing and understitch (see page 29) close to the previous seam, catching the seam allowances underneath as you go.

6 Press the facing to the inside and tack it in place 3 cm (1¼ in.) from the neck edge. Topstitch from the right side, close to the tacking. On the inside, trim the facing close to the topstitching.

7 Open the garment out and lay it flat. With right sides together, matching the small dot on the sleeve to the shoulder seam and matching the notches on the front and back of the top, pin the sleeve to the armhole edge. Stitch, then press the seam towards the sleeve. Repeat for the other sleeve.

8 With right sides together, pin the front and back together at the sleeves and sides. Stitch from the outer edge of the sleeve and down the sides, leaving a gap between the circles on the lower edges of the seam, as shown. Clip the seam allowance 1 cm (⅜ in.) above the upper circle. Press the seams towards the back.

9 Turn the lower edge of the garment to the right side, matching the circles, and pin in place. Stitch below the circles on either side, as shown.

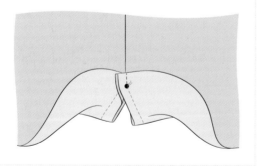

10 Turn the hem allowance to the inside, making a 7-cm (2¾-in.) hem, and stitch in place close to the raw edge.

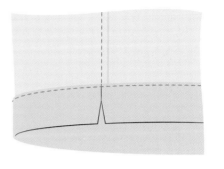

11 Turn up the sleeve hem by 2 cm (¾ in.) and pin and stitch in place close to the inner edge.

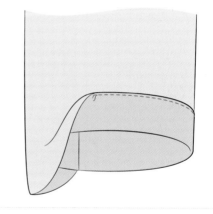

HACK

BRETON TEE

Using the same pattern pieces as the Breton Top, but leaving out the sleeves, this summer top can be made up using a comfortable stretch fabric. A simple T-shirt such as this can be made so many times in different fabrics to create a variety of looks. Try it in a sparkling jersey for evening or a graphic print to team with plain trousers.

MATERIALS
1 m (1 yd) fabric, 150 cm (60 in.) wide

25 cm (10 in.) cotton stay tape, 6 mm (¼ in.) wide

Matching sewing thread

Ballpoint needle

Basic sewing kit (see page 10)

DIFFICULTY LEVEL
Beginner

FABRIC SUGGESTIONS
Cotton or viscose jersey.

DESIGN NOTES
Use a 1.5-cm (⅝-in.) seam allowance throughout.

FINISHED MEASUREMENTS	8	10	12	14	16	18	20
BUST (cm)	107	112	117	122	128	134	140
BUST (in.)	42⅛	44⅛	46¹⁄₁₆	48	50⅜	52¾	55⅛
WAIST (cm)	79.5	84.5	89.5	94.5	100.5	106.5	112.5
WAIST (in.)	31¼	33¼	35¼	37¼	39½	41⅞	44¼

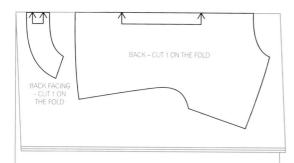

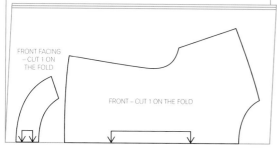

LAYOUT PLAN

Trace off the pattern pieces – front, back, front facing and back facing. All pieces are cut on the fold. After preparing your fabric, fold it right sides together, with the selvedges meeting in the middle, and lay out the pattern pieces as shown. Measure to the selvedge to make sure that the grain is straight. Cut out and transfer any markings to the fabric (see Get Set to Sew, page 21).

MAKE UP THE TOP

Make up following the instructions for the Breton Top on page 93, but omitting step 7.

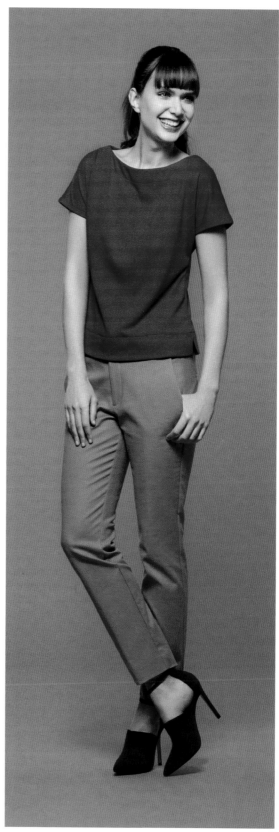

HACK

JERSEY DRESS

This longer-length version of the Breton Top on pages 92–97 makes the perfect pull-on stretch dress – a staple garment in almost every woman's wardrobe.

MATERIALS
2.5 m (2¾ yd) fabric, 150 cm (60 in.) wide

25 cm (10 in.) cotton stay tape, 6 mm (¼ in.) wide

Matching sewing thread

Ballpoint needle

Basic sewing kit (see page 10)

DIFFICULTY LEVEL
Beginner

FABRIC SUGGESTIONS
Cotton or viscose jersey.

DESIGN NOTES
This design is a very simple T-shirt dress with three-quarter length sleeves and a round neckline. Because it has been stitched in a stretch jersey, there is no need for any additional opening or fastening.

Use a 1.5-cm (⅝-in.) seam allowance throughout.

FINISHED MEASUREMENTS	8	10	12	14	16	18	20
BUST (cm)	107	112	117	122	128	134	140
BUST (in.)	42⅛	44⅛	46¹⁄₁₆	48	50⅜	52¾	55⅛
WAIST (cm)	79.5	84.5	89.5	94.5	100.5	106.5	112.5
WAIST (in.)	31¼	33¼	35¼	37¼	39½	41⅞	44¼
HIP (cm)	94.5	99.5	104.5	109.5	115.5	121.5	127.5
HIP (in.)	37¼	39	41	43	45½	47¾	50

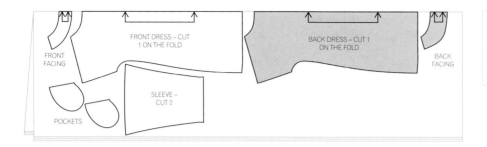

FRONT FACING

FRONT DRESS – CUT
1 ON THE FOLD

BACK DRESS – CUT 1
ON THE FOLD

BACK
FACING

FRONT FACING –
CUT 1 ON THE FOLD
BACK FACING – CUT
1 ON THE FOLD
POCKET – CUT 4

SLEEVE –
CUT 2

POCKETS

LAYOUT
PLAN

Trace off the pattern pieces –
front, back, sleeve, front facing,
back facing and pockets. The
front, back and facings are all cut
on the fold. After preparing your
fabric, fold it right sides together,
and lay out the pattern pieces as
shown. Measure to the selvedge
to make sure that the grain is
straight. For the sleeves, fold the
fabric in half widthways, with the
selvedges together. Cut out and
transfer markings to the fabric
(see Get Set to Sew, page 21).

1 MAKE UP THE DRESS
Make up the dress, following steps 1–7 of
the Breton Top on page 93.

2 With right sides together, matching the
dots, pin and sew the pockets onto the
front dress sides, sewing between the
marked points only. Repeat to sew pocket
pieces to the dress back.

3 Working from the right side, press the
pockets and seam allowances away from
the front and back dress pieces and then
understitch between the dots on the pocket
side of the seam line, not on the front dress.

4 With right sides together, making sure
the raw edges and pockets align, lay
the back dress over the front dress.
Pin along the sleeve seams, side seams and
around the pockets. Machine stitch from the
sleeve down to the hem in one continuous line
of stitching, pivoting at the previously stitched
points around the pockets.

5 Press under a 1.5-cm (⅝-in.) hem around
the sleeve ends. Working from the right
side, pin and machine the hem in place.

6 Hem the bottom of the dress in the same
way as the sleeves, pressing under a
2.5-cm (1-in.) hem.

DESIGNER TIPS
WORKING WITH STRETCH FABRICS

Working with stretch fabrics can be tricky, but there are a few things that will make it easier to handle.

• When sewing, use a walking or an evenfeed foot – this will mean the fabric goes through the machine evenly.

• Use a ballpoint needle, which has a slightly rounded tip that parts the fibres rather than pierces them. Using a ballpoint or stretch needle will create an even stitch without breaking the fibres.

• Many sewing machines have a stretch stitch (which looks like a flash of lightening). This means that the seam will stretch along with the fabric and not break. If your machine doesn't have a stretch stitch, you can use a small zigzag.

• Stretch fabrics do not fray, so you don't need to finish the edges; however, they could be neatened with an overlocker. If you are not overlocking, then stitch each seam twice and trim close to the second stitching before pressing.

• To stabilise the edge before completing the hem, cut strips of fusible stretch interfacing the width of the finished hem. Fuse in place right up to the raw edge, then complete the hem.

• Use a twin needle for a professional-looking hem finish.

For more information on stretch fabrics, see page 176.

PEPLUM DRESS

PEPLUM DRESS

A peplum adds flare and detail to a simple silhouette, creating the
illusion of a smaller waist, whilst hiding the hips and tummy.
What's not to love? With a body-hugging bodice and slimline skirt, this
dress looks striking made up in an African-inspired waxed cotton.

MATERIALS
3.5 m (3⅞ yd) medium-weight cotton,
115 cm (45 in.) wide

25 cm (10 in.) iron-on interfacing

45-cm (18-in.) invisible zip

Matching sewing thread

Basic sewing kit (see page 10)

DIFFICULTY LEVEL
Intermediate

FABRIC SUGGESTIONS
We've used a waxed cotton, but this
design works equally well in a medium-
weight cotton, gabardine, satin-backed
crepe or lightweight wool.

DESIGN NOTES
The bodice is fitted, with bust and waist
darts, and finished with an invisible zip
in the centre back, extending into the
shaped peplum. The pencil skirt is knee
skimming with a back slit for ease when
walking. The short sleeves mirror the
shaping on the overlapping peplum.

Use a 1.5-cm (⅝-in.) seam allowance.

FINISHED MEASUREMENTS	8	10	12	14	16	18	20
BUST (cm)	86	91	96	101	107	113	119
BUST (in.)	33⅞	35⅞	37¾	39¾	42⅛	44½	46⅞
WAIST (cm)	67.5	72.5	77.5	82.5	88.5	94.5	100.5
WAIST (in.)	26½	28½	30½	32½	34⅞	37¼	39½
HIP (cm)	94.5	99.5	104.5	109.5	115.5	121.5	127.5
HIP (in.)	37¼	39⅛	41⅛	43⅛	45½	47¾	50⅛

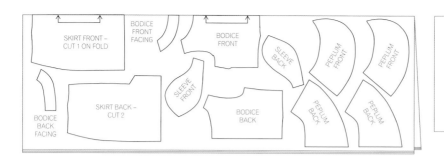

SKIRT FRONT –
CUT 1 ON FOLD

BODICE
FRONT
FACING

BODICE
FRONT

SLEEVE
BACK

PEPLUM
FRONT

PEPLUM
FRONT

SLEEVE
FRONT

SKIRT BACK –
CUT 2

BODICE
BACK

PEPLUM
BACK

PEPLUM
BACK

BODICE
BACK
FACING

BODICE FRONT – CUT 1 ON FOLD
BODICE BACK – CUT 2
SLEEVE BACK – CUT 2
SLEEVE FRONT – CUT 2
PEPLUM BACK – CUT 4
PEPLUM FRONT – CUT 4
BODICE FRONT FACING – CUT 1 IN
FABRIC AND 1 IN INTERFACING
BODICE BACK FACING – CUT 2 IN
FABRIC AND 2 IN INTERFACING

LAYOUT PLAN

Trace off the pattern pieces – bodice front, bodice back, skirt front, skirt back, sleeve front, sleeve back, peplum front, peplum back, bodice front facing and bodice back facing. After preparing your fabric, fold it in half widthways, right sides together, and lay out the pattern pieces as shown. Measure to the selvedge to make sure that the grain is straight. Cut out and transfer any markings to the fabric (see Get Set to Sew, page 21). Note that the peplum pieces are cut twice – the second pieces are for the lining. Alternatively, the second pieces could be cut from a lining fabric.

2 Fold the bust darts on the bodice front by folding the fabric right sides together, matching the dart markings. Tack and stitch from the side seam, tapering to the fold of the fabric at the tip and taking the last two or three stitches right on the fold. Do not backstitch; instead, leave thread tails and tie off the ends. Press the bust darts over a ham (see Darts, page 150). Press the darts downwards.

1 MAKE THE BODICE
Staystitch (see page 29) the bodice front and back neck edges 13 mm (½ in.) from the edge, stitching with a regular 2.5 stitch length just inside the seam allowance and stitching from the shoulder to the centre of the bodice each time.

3 Fold the waist darts on the back and front bodices by folding the fabric right sides together, matching the dart markings. Tack and stitch from the widest part (at the waist seam) towards the tip, tapering to stitch the last two or three stitches right on the fold. Press the darts towards the centre of the bodice.

TIP

If using a fabric with a one-way print, make sure that all pattern pieces are laid out the same way on the fabric, top to bottom.

4 With right sides together, pin and stitch the bodice front to the bodice back pieces at the shoulder seams. Pin and stitch the bodice side seams. Press the seams open and neaten the raw edges. Set the bodice to one side.

5 **MAKE THE SKIRT**
Fold, tack and stitch the waist darts in the skirt front and back sections, as in step 3. With right sides together, sew the skirt backs to the front at the side seams. (The skirt back is not stitched together until after the zip has been inserted.)

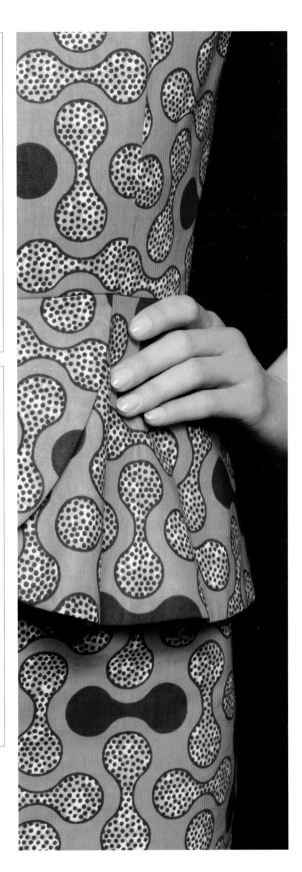

CORE SKILL
Invisible (concealed) zip

An invisible or concealed zip is sewn in place without any stitching being visible on the right side of the garment. It differs from a regular zip, as the teeth are on the underside of the zip tape with just the little zip pull on the right side. Use a special invisible zip foot.

1 Neaten the edges of the seam allowances and press. Then fold the seam allowances to the wrong side along the seam lines and press to form a crease. (An invisible zip is inserted before the seam is stitched.)

2 Open out the seam allowances. With the fabric right side up, place the opened zip face down on the seam allowance, with the teeth along the crease. Pin and tack in place, to the seam allowance only, positioning the zip so that the teeth start at least 1.5 cm (⅝ in.) below the top edge of the fabric.

3 Attach the invisible zip foot, with the needle in the centre position so it will go through the small hole in the foot. Place the fabric under the foot so that the zip teeth slip into one of the grooves on the underside of the foot and the needle will stitch into the zip tape next to the teeth. As you stitch, gently uncurl the zip teeth so that the stitching is under the teeth. Stitch as close to the bottom as possible. Reverse stitch to secure.

4 Close the zip and check you have stitched close enough to the teeth (you should not be able to see any of the zip tape on the stitched side). If not, simply stitch again, moving the needle a tad closer to the teeth. Then bring the garment sections right sides together and pin the zip tape to the seam allowance as before, with the zip teeth along the crease made earlier, then open the zip and unpin the garment sections, just keeping the zip pinned to the seam allowance.

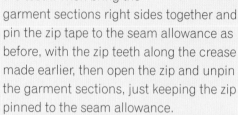

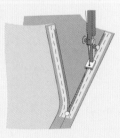

5 With the second garment piece right side up, tack the zip to the seam allowance. Again stitch from top to bottom, with the teeth running through the other groove in the invisible zip foot and the needle very close to the teeth.

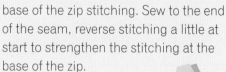

6 Change back to your regular zip foot. Pin the rest of the seam together and then start stitching 1–2 mm (about ⅟₁₆ in.) to the left of and 6 mm (¼ in.) above the base of the zip stitching. Sew to the end of the seam, reverse stitching a little at start to strengthen the stitching at the base of the zip.

7 Finish by stitching the ends of the zip tape to the seam allowances only on either side of the zip to keep them from flapping about. Remove any tacking stitches. Press.

6 MAKE THE PEPLUM

With right sides together, stitch a peplum back to a peplum front piece at the sides along the notched short edge. Press the seam open. Repeat for the peplum lining. With right sides together, matching the seams, pin the main fabric peplum to the peplum lining along the un-notched edge. Stitch along the centre back edge and along the lower edge of the peplum up to the front. Trim the seam allowance and clip off the corners. Clip around the curve.

7

Press the seam towards the lining and understitch through the lining and seam allowances close to the previous seam, as far as possible.

8

Turn the peplum right side out and press. Tack the raw edges of the top of the peplum together. Repeat with the remaining peplum pieces.

9

Turn the skirt right side out. Pin the left peplum to the skirt at the front waistline, matching the markings on the waistline, and then pin around to the back centre seam. Tack in place. Repeat for the right peplum piece, matching the markings on the waistline and overlapping the left peplum at the centre front.

10 ATTACH THE BODICE TO THE SKIRT

With right sides together, matching the centre front, waist darts and side seams, slip the bodice over the peplum and skirt and pin all layers together around the waist edges. Stitch in place, trim the seam allowance and press the seam towards the bodice.

11 ATTACH THE FACING

Fuse interfacing to the wrong side of the facing pieces. Once cool, stitch the back facing pieces to the front facing at the short ends and press the seams open. Then neaten the outer edge of the facing by overlocking, overedge stitching or turning a narrow hem (see page 43).

12 With right sides together, matching the shoulder seams and the centre front and back edges, pin the facing to the neck edge of the bodice. Stitch in place. Trim seam allowance, clipping at the curves.

13 Press the seam allowance towards the facing, then understitch through the facing, close to the seam,

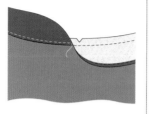

catching the seam allowances underneath. Turn the facing to the inside and press. Hand stitch the facing in place at shoulder seams.

14 Insert the invisible zip in the centre back seam, with the top of the zip teeth close to the top of the neckline (open out the facing and pin the peplum back out of the way). (See page 108 for invisible zip insertion). Stitch the seam as far as the large dot marking the skirt vent.

15 Reinforce the inner corner of the vent and stitch the upper end of the vent extension by starting 2.5 cm (1 in.) above the large dot on the seam line, stitching to the

dot, and then pivoting and stitching across the upper end of the extensions. Clip diagonally back to the dot at the inner corner. Press the seam open above the clip. Neaten the raw edges by turning a double narrow hem and topstitching.

16 Press the vent extension towards the left back and tack it in place. On the right side of the garment, stitch the left back along the tacking, as shown.

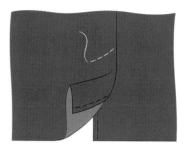

17 At the top of the zip, tuck the upper ends of the zipper tape inside and fold the facing back down. Slipstitch the facing to the zip tape.

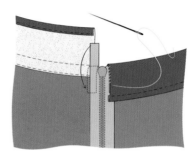

18 INSERT THE SLEEVES
With right sides together, matching the notches, stitch the sleeve front to the sleeve back at the underarms (the straight edges). Press the seam open. Turn under and press a 1-cm (⅜-in.) hem on the lower edge of the joined pieces, tucking the raw edge under to meet the crease. Topstitch the hem in place.

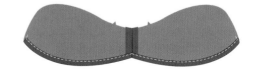

19 Working from the right side, lap the front sleeve over the back, matching the small dots. Tack the raw edges together. Ease stitch (stitch with a slightly longer 3.5–4 stitch length on the seam line and 6 mm/¼ in. from the raw edge) between the notches.

20 With the sleeve right side out, hold the bodice wrong side out with the armhole towards you. With right sides together, pin the sleeve to the armhole edge, matching the centre dot on the sleeve to the shoulder seam and the underarm seam to the bodice side seam. Pull up the bobbin thread of the ease stitches to fit the sleeve head, distributing the fullness evenly until there are no puckers on the seamline. Tack and machine stitch. Stitch again 3 mm (⅛ in.) from first row but within the seam allowance. Trim the seam allowance and press the seam allowance only with steam to shrink out any fullness. Repeat steps 18–20 for the second sleeve.

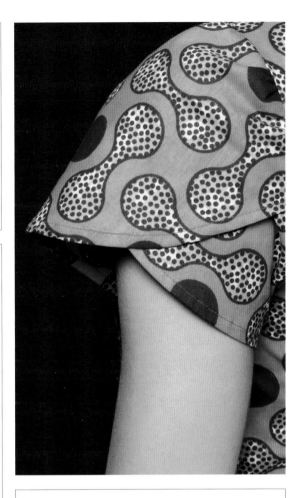

21 HEM THE DRESS
Let the garment hang for 24 hours. Mark the length and open out the left back extension. Press up the hem allowance along the marking and trim the hem allowance depth evenly if necessary. Neaten the raw edge of the hem allowance with an overedge stitch or overlocker. Finish the hem by hand, slipstitching it or blind hemming by machine. Press the left back vent to the inside and slipstitch it to the hem.

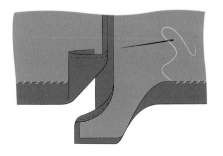

HACK

WIGGLE SKIRT

Fancy a quick sewing fix? Make this simple stretch wiggle skirt in just a couple of hours using the pencil skirt pattern pieces from the Peplum Dress project (pages 104–111). We've made this with an overlocker, but you can also sew this skirt on a regular sewing machine with a narrow zigzag stitch.

MATERIALS
1 m (1 yd) fabric, 115 or 150 cm (45 or 60 in.) wide

Matching sewing thread

1 m (40 in.) elastic, 4 cm (1½ in.) wide

Twin needle

Basic sewing kit (see page 10)

DIFFICULTY LEVEL
Beginner

FABRIC SUGGESTIONS
Stable double-knit jersey such as Ponte Roma, warm jersey, etc. Not suitable for woven fabric, Lycra or any fabric with an excessive amount of stretch.

DESIGN NOTES
A wiggle skirt is a slim-fitting skirt with enough stretch to give that 'Marilyn' effect when walking. This version has an elasticated waist and a centre back seam. You can make it any length to suit your personal style – as a mini skirt, knee skimming or mid calf.

Use a 1-cm (⅜-in.) seam allowance unless otherwise stated.

FINISHED MEASUREMENTS	8	10	12	14	16	18	20
WAIST (cm)	65.5	70.5	75.5	80.5	86.5	92.5	98.5
WAIST (in.)	25¾	27¾	29¾	31⅝	34	36⅜	39¾
HIP (cm)	92.5	97.5	102.5	107.5	113.5	119.5	125.5
HIP (in.)	36⅜	38⅜	40⅜	42⅛	44⅝	47	49⅜

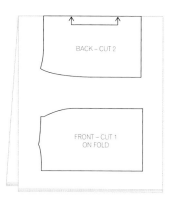

LAYOUT PLAN

Trace off the pattern pieces in your size, but then remove the 1.5-cm (⅝-in.) seam allowances from the side seams and the centre back seam. As we are using stretch fabric we do not need the darts at the front and back of the skirt. To remove them, simply fold and pin the darts in the tissue pieces. Press flat. Use these as the pattern pieces to cut out the stretch fabric. Adjust the pattern piece for the skirt back in the same way, dividing the width of the dart between the centre back seam and the side seam. Adjust the pattern pieces along the lengthen/shorten line. Make sure that the greatest direction of stretch runs horizontally around the skirt rather than vertically. Cut out and transfer any markings to the fabric.

1 With right sides together, pin the two skirt backs together along the centre back seam. Stitch, using an overlocker or a narrow zigzag stitch on a sewing machine. With right sides together, pin the skirt front to the skirt back along the side seams. Stitch, using an overlocker or a narrow zigzag stitch.

2 Try on your skirt, making sure it is inside out, to check the fit. Adjust and pin the side seams and the back seam, until you get the perfect fit for you.

3 Measure a piece of elastic around your waistline and mark the length. Add a 2.5-cm (1-in.) overlap, then cut the elastic to the length required. Overlap the ends of the elastic to form a ring and sew two parallel rows of vertical lines of stitching to hold it together. Divide both waist of the skirt and the prepared elastic into quarters and mark these points with pins.

4 Pin the elastic to the wrong side (inside) of the skirt waist, matching the pins and aligning the top edge of the elastic with the raw edge of the waistline. Using either an overlocker or a narrow zigzag stitch, stitch the upper edge of the elastic to the waistband, evenly stretching the elastic to fit the fabric.

5 Fold the elastic to the wrong side of the skirt and pin. With the skirt right side out, stitch over the hem edge of the elastic, using a twin needle for stretch fabric. Turn up the hem allowance to required length, tucking raw edge under again. Working from the right side, use a ball-point twin needle and top stitch the hem in place.

CORE SKILL
Blind hemming

A blind hem is not supposed to be visible from the outside at all, although a machine-stitched blind hem may leave a trace of tiny ladder-like stitches.

BLIND HEM BY MACHINE

To minimise the visibility on the right side, use a thread colour in both bobbin and needle that closely matches the garment. A blind hem stitch is created by a few straight stitches, then one zigzag stitch to the left. It is also preferable to use a blind hem foot. This has a vertical guide in the centre protruding below the foot, against which the hem allowance fold is butted.

Prior to stitching the hem in place, whether by hand or machine, it is advisable to finish the raw edge by overcasting or zigzag stitching close to the edge and then trimming close to the stitching. Fabrics that do not fray, such as stretch knits and fleece, do not need neatening.

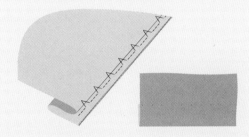

1 Fold up the hem allowance and pin at right angles to the hem edge.

2 Fold the hem allowance back on itself so that about 1 cm (⅜ in.) of the neatened hem edge is visible on the right-hand side.

3 Snap on the blind hem foot and place the hem under the foot so that the folded edge is against the vertical guide on the foot.

4 Select the blind hem stitch and test stitch. The straight stitch should be on the hem allowance only and the zigzag just catching into the fold. If it takes too big a stitch into the fold, reduce the stitch width and try again. Once you are happy with the positioning, stitch your hem.

5 Once complete, fold the hem back to the wrong side and press carefully to set the stitches, avoiding pressing the hem edge which should be left soft and rounded.

BLIND HEM BY HAND

Use a thread colour to match the garment.

1 Turn up the hem at hem level, pinning it in place parallel to the fold, with any seams matching.

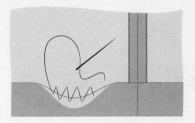

2 Starting at a seam, fold back 13 mm (½ in.) of the hem allowance and hold it folded down with one hand. Secure the thread to the seam allowance of the seam, then bring the thread up through the folded-back hem allowance. Take the needle through to the garment and pick up just one or two fibres of the garment fabric before bringing needle back through the folded hem allowance approximately 6–13 mm (¼–½ in.) in front of the last stitch. Continue in this manner along the hem, allowing the folded-back hem allowance to fall back in place as you go.

SARI INTO DRESS

SARI INTO DRESS

Sari fabrics are wonderful lengths of fabric from which to make your own bespoke garments. The challenge on *The Great British Sewing Bee* was to transform a sari within 90 minutes, but you can take your time to create this pleated dress with a kimono-inspired bodice.

MATERIALS
1 sari length

2 m (2 yd) lightweight cotton or polyester lining fabric for interlining

40-cm (16-in.) zip

Hook-and-eye fastener

Matching thread

Basic sewing kit (see page 10)

DIFFICULTY LEVEL
Intermediate

FABRIC SUGGESTIONS
You can, of course, make this dress from any fabric. You will need approx 3.2 m (3½ yd) of fabric to do so. Choose a fabric that will pleat nicely, such as a cotton, linen look or polyester.

DESIGN NOTES
This dress has been made without a pattern, rather it has been created from a sari length cut into a full pleated skirt, a midriff section and a bodice cut from two simple rectangles to create a kimono-inspired top. Sometimes sari fabrics are very transparent, which may require you to either interline the dress or to wear with a full-length slip. The dress is finished with a lapped zip at the centre back.

A sari length can be 5–8 m (5½–8¾ yd) long and is generally 107–124 cm (42–49 in.) wide. It usually has an ornamental border along the selvedges and a matching end piece, called the pallu, which is worn as the drape over the shoulder or head. There is often an additional piece of co-ordinating fabric on the end of the sari for the choli, or tight-fitting cropped blouse that is frequently worn with the sari.

Use a 1.5-cm (⅝-in.) seam allowance, unless otherwise stated.

CORE SKILL
Perfect Pleats

Pleats are quite simply folds in the fabric used to provide shaping, as a design detail or to take out excess fabric. Because they are created by folding the fabric, more fabric is required than normal. The amount will depend on the number and depth of the pleat.

PLEAT STYLES

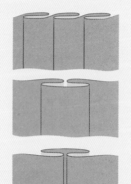

There are three main pleat types: knife, box and inverted. Knife pleats are the most common type, these are straight pleats, all facing the same direction. A box pleat is really two knife pleats turned away from each other to form a straight panel with a pleat either side. If you turn the box pleat to the reverse, it will form an inverted pleat. An inverted pleat is formed by two straight pleats again, but this time turned towards each other to form a V-shaped opening. Kick pleats are a variation of the inverted pleat and may have the underlay section cut from a contrast fabric to add a design detail.

PLEAT TEMPLATE

To ensure that multiple pleats are even, use a pleat template, which is easy to make from a strip of card. Having determined the width of the fabric to be taken in the pleat, cut a card strip to this width. On one long edge, mark 'Placement Line'; on the other long edge, mark 'Fold Line'. Place the card on the right side of the fabric to be pleated and mark the two lines, using a different colour for each.

CREATING PLEATS

1 Fold the fabric at the Fold Line mark and bring it to the Placement Line mark, keeping the upper edges of the fabric even. The pleat formed will be half the width of the marked fabric. Repeat along the top edge to create as many pleats as desired.

2 For unpressed pleats, mark down the folds from the top edge by 5–10 cm (2–4 in.). For crisp, pressed pleats, mark the whole pleat length so they can be pressed in neatly.

3 Stitch across the top of the pleats to hold them in place, stitching just inside the seam line. If desired, you can also stitch down the first 5–10 cm (2–4 in.) to keep the top of the pleated fabric flat (for instance, to reduce bulk around the waist). To do this, stitch very close to the folded edge of the pleat.

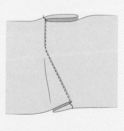

4 To keep pleats folded in place, working from the wrong side, machine stitch close to the inner fold, particularly in the hem area.

5 Press. (Always use a press cloth when pressing pleats to avoid leaving fold imprints on the garment.)

1 MARK AND CUT OUT THE PIECES

For the skirt, use the full width of the sari fabric and cut a piece that is three times your waist measurement along the length.

2

Measure the length you want the skirt to be from waist to hem line and add 1.5 cm (⅝ in.) for the hem allowance. Mark this length from either the top selvedge to the required hem or from the decorative edge of the panel up. Cut across the panel.

TIP

If your sari has a heavy border trim, hand stitch some of the trim along the neck edge.

Use another length as a belt, turning the raw ends to the underside and stitching them down and then adding hooks and eyes as fasteners.

TIP

Fold the skirt piece in half widthways and pin the layers together to hold them in place. Mark the length and cut through the two layers of fabric at once.

3

From the remaining sari fabric, cut two rectangles 30 cm wide x 75 cm long (12 x 29½ in.) for the bodice. For the midriff band cut a strip 9 cm (3½ in.) wide multiplied by your under bust measurement. If you are interlining the dress, cut the bodice and midriff sections in interlining, too.

4

For the skirt lining, divide your waist measurement by four and add 5 cm (2 in.) for the seam allowance/ease. Fold the fabric right sides and selvedges together and draw out the pattern for the skirt front. Draw across the top from the fold to the quarter waist measurement plus 5 cm (2 in.), then mark the skirt length down the fold. From this point, draw a horizontal line 55 cm (21½ in.) long. Draw the side seamline from the top of the waist diagonally down to the marked line by the length required. Curve the hem edge from fold to side seam to get the required length. For the back of the skirt, use the front as a template, flipping it over and positioning the straight edge 1.5 cm (⅝ in.) from the selvedges. When you draw the horizontal line, extend it as far as the selvedge to allow for a centre back seam allowance. Cut out the two back sections.

BACK –
CUT 2

FRONT –
CUT ON FOLD

5 MAKE THE SKIRT

With right sides together, pin the skirt panel short ends together for 15 cm (6 in.) down from the waist, then machine sew the rest of the seam (this will be the centre back seam). Neaten the raw edges of the seam allowances separately.

6

Find the centre front of the skirt panel along the top edge and pin mark. Then find and pin mark the middle of the fabric between the centre back seam and the centre front along the top edge. Do this on both sides.

7

To make the centre pleat, measure out either side of the centre front mark by 10 cm (4 in.) and pin mark. Make a fold at the outer pin marks and bring both folds to the centre pin mark to create an inverted pleat.

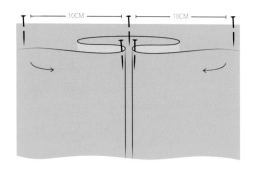

8

Make and pin baste equal-sized knife pleats, approximately 4–5 cm (1½–2 in.) deep, facing towards the centre pleat on either side all the way around the top edge of the skirt to the centre back seam, leaving the last 5 cm (2 in.) unpleated (see page 118.) Slip the skirt on to check the size. If necessary, adjust the pleats to accommodate more or less fabric. Machine baste across the top of the pleats to keep them in place.

9

Make up the skirt lining by stitching the side seams and centre back seam, starting 15 cm (6 in.) from the top edge. Neaten all the seam allowances, including the waist seam allowance.

10

With the skirt right side out, pin the lining inside around the top edge, with the right side of the lining against the wrong side of the skirt, matching the centre front of the lining with the inverted pleat and matching the centre back seams. If necessary, take little pleats in the lining top edge about 10 cm (4 in.) from the centre back seam to allow a little ease in the lining. Stitch around the top edge, taking a 1-cm (⅜-in.) seam allowance.

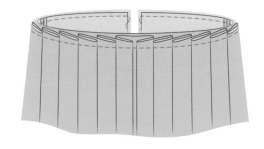

11 MAKE THE MIDRIFF SECTION
If you are using an interlining,
pin and stitch the wrong side of
the interlining to the reverse of the midriff
section along one long edge to hold the layers
together. Neaten the stitched edge with zigzag
or overedge stitch.

12 With right sides together, pin and
stitch the neatened edge of the
midriff to the top edge of the skirt.
Press the seam allowances up towards
the bodice.

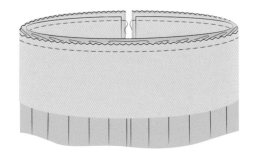

13 Grade (see page 43) the seam
allowances to reduce the bulk at the
seam: keeping the skirt lining seam
allowance out of the way, carefully trim back
the sari skirt and the midriff seam allowances
to a scant 6 mm (¼ in.). Pin the sari midriff
fabric out of the way, and then machine
stitch the skirt lining seam allowance to the
interlining of the midriff, effectively enclosing
the trimmed seam allowances inside.

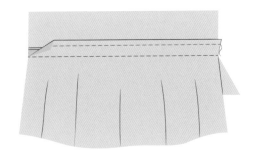

14 Fold the sari midriff piece back
up and machine stitch the sides
and top edge to hold the layers
together. Neaten the raw edges by zigzag or
overedge stitching.

15 MAKE THE BODICE
If you are using interlining, pin the
wrong side of the interlining to the
wrong side of the bodice pieces and stitch
in place down both long edges. Stitch again
close to the first row of stitching and trim the
seam close. Turn through and press.

CORE SKILL
Lapped zip

A lapped zip has taken over from the centre zip as the most popular way to insert a zip. It has one edge of fabric lapping the other, so that only one row of stitching is visible. The other edge is stitched very close to the zip teeth. Often used in side seams, it is also used at centre back seams.

1 Neaten the raw edges of the seam allowances into which the zip is to be placed. Press to embed the stitching.

2 Mark the zip position and machine baste the zip seam closed, using the longest stitch length available. Reduce the stitch length to a regular 2.5 and machine stitch the rest of the seam, reverse stitching at the start and end of the seam. Press the seam open.

3 With the zip open and face down, tack the zip tape to the left-hand seam allowance only, tacking along the outer edge of the zip tape, with the teeth of the zip along the seam.

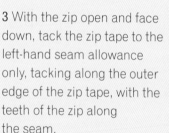

4 Close the zip and turn so that the zip is right side up and the left seam allowance is folded along the zip teeth, with just a tiny amount (2–3 mm/⅛ in.) of seam allowance visible. Attach your zip foot and machine as close to the teeth as possible on the tiny bit of seam allowance. If necessary move the needle to the right a little, with the

narrow edge of the zip foot running along the folded edge of the fabric closest to the teeth.

5 Snip into the seam allowance below the zip end.

6 Working on a flat surface and with the garment right side down, check that the zip lies flat. Then pin and tack the right side of the zip tape

through all layers, starting at the bottom. Tack across the bottom and up the side, 6 mm (¼ in.) from the centre of the teeth.

7 Turn the work over so that the right side is uppermost. Machine stitch across the bottom and up the side as before, 6–10 mm

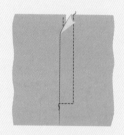

(¼–⅜ in.) from the teeth. (The distance depends on the thickness of the fabric: finer fabrics can be stitched closer to the teeth; fleece or woollens should be stitched further from the teeth.) Remove the tacking stitches.

TIP
To ensure a straight line of stitching, draw a chalk line along the stitching line, or place masking tape alongside the stitching line.

16 With right sides together, fold each bodice rectangle in half widthways. The fold will be the shoulder seam. Mark from the open end up the side seams by 23 cm (9 in.) and pin the seam. Try on to check the armhole is the right size for you – lengthen or shorten the side seam if needed and check that the side seams are in line with your body. The centre front edges of the two bodice pieces will be joined with a seam and the centre back edges with a zip. If needed, take in the sides by angling down from armhole opening to the bottom edge. Sew both the side seams.

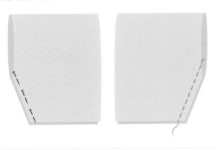

18 Gather stitch the lower front and back bodice sections, stopping and starting 5 cm (2 in.) either side of the front and side seams. Alternatively, stitch darts from lower edge to bust, stopping 2.5 cm (1 in.) below the bust point. Do the same on the back. To gather, use the longest machine stitch available and stitch, leaving long thread tails. Pull up the bobbin thread to gather the fabric.

17 Pin the centre front edges of the bodice pieces right sides together. Measure and mark about 18 cm (7 in.) up from the lower edge. Starting at the lower edge and using a 1-cm (⅜-in.) seam allowance, stitch the bodices together, tapering to the fabric edge as you stitch the last 2 cm (¾ in.). Press the seam open.

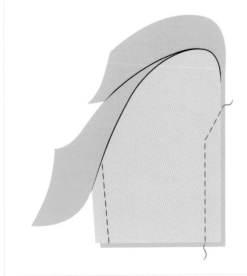

19 ATTACH THE BODICE TO THE MIDRIFF
With right sides together, matching the centre fronts and centre backs, pin the bodice to the midriff. Take tiny pleats or gather the bodice front and back a little to ease in fullness to fit the midriff panel. You may also have to trim the lower edge to shape it (depending on your bust size and how much the front edge rises). Pin and stitch together. Trim the seams and neaten the raw edges. Press the seam allowance down towards the midriff.

20 INSERT THE ZIP

Tack the centre back edges of the bodice pieces together, starting approx. 18 cm (7 in.) above the midriff band. Press the seam open. Following the instructions on page 122, insert a lapped zip into the back seam. At the top of the zip, hand stitch a hook-and-eye fastener.

21 HEM THE DRESS

Allow the garment to hang overnight to let the side seams settle if necessary. Straighten the hem edge and finish the hem by your chosen method. (A rolled hem is perfect for transparent fabrics.) Hem the skirt lining with a double-turned topstitched hem, making it shorter than the garment by 2 cm (¾ in.).

TIP

If you have used the border sari edge at the hem you will not need to hem the skirt.

DESIGNER TIPS
FOR SEWING LIGHTWEIGHT FABRICS

• When handling lightweight fabrics, such as sari silks and polyesters, avoid them getting pulled into the throat plate at the start of seams using one of the following methods:

1 Start 1 cm (⅜ in.) from the end, stitch two or three stitches forward and then reverse to the start of the fabric, holding the thread tails, continue forward again to the end of the seam.

2 Place a little soluble stabiliser or tissue paper underneath the fabric at the start of the seam, which can be washed or torn away afterwards.

• Prevent 'bird nesting'. Avoid threads tangling together at the start of the seam, which can pucker fabric or just look unsightly, by holding both needle and bobbin thread taut in your left hand as you start to sew. Hold until at least 2.5 cm (1 in.) has been sewn.

• Make sure you use a new, universal sharps needle, size 70/9 to avoid seams puckering.

1960s COLOUR-BLOCKED DRESS

1960s COLOUR-BLOCKED DRESS

The Mondrian cocktail dress by YSL, which was made in slippery crepe de chine, is considered one of the most significant dresses of the 20th century. Our simpler version is inspired by the original and made from cotton.Colour blocking is as on trend now as it was in the 1960s.

MATERIALS
In total, the dress needs approx. 2 m (2⅛ yards) of fabric. Use a fabric that is 115 cm (45 in.) wide:

1 m (1⅛ yd) white fabric (panels 3 and 5)

40 cm (½ yd) green fabric (panel 1)

40 cm (½ yd) navy blue fabric (panel 9)

70 cm (⅝ yd) yellow fabric (panel 7)

60 cm (⅝ yd) black fabric (panels 2, 4, 6 and 8)

55-cm (22-in.) dress zip

Matching sewing thread

Basic sewing kit (see page 10)

DIFFICULTY LEVEL
Beginner/Intermediate

FABRIC SUGGESTIONS
Light- or medium-weight cottons and cotton blends, cotton sateen, medium-weight double knits like a fine ponte di Roma, crepe de chine, lightweight wool blends, silk shantung, lightweight duchess satin.

DESIGN NOTES
Cut all the front pieces with both the fabric and the pattern piece right side up. Number each piece with a chalk pencil on the back so they are easily identified when you put them together. Press all seams before sewing over them again.

Use a 1.5-cm (⅝-in.) seam allowance throughout, unless otherwise stated.

FINISHED MEASUREMENTS	8	10	12	14	16	18	20
BUST (cm)	88.75	93.75	98.75	103.75	109.75	115.75	121.75
BUST (in.)	34⅞	36⅞	38⅞	40⅞	43¼	45½	47⅞
WAIST (cm)	82.75	87.75	92.75	97.75	103.75	109.75	115.75
WAIST (in.)	32½	34½	36½	38½	40⅞	43¼	45½
HIP (cm)	96.75	101.75	106.75	111.75	117.75	123.75	129.75
HIP (in.)	38	40	42	44	46⅜	48¾	51⅛

CORE SKILL
Bias binding

Bias binding not only finishes the edges of a garment beautifully but also neatly encases the raw edges. Bound edges look great on necklines, sleeveless armholes and edge-to-edge jackets. They are ideal on garments where the reverse will show, as the edges are all neat and uniform, and on transparent fabrics where any facings would show through.

Bindings are usually made from bias-cut strips of fabric, so that they will bend around curved areas easily and without ripples. Bias binding can be purchased ready made in a variety of widths and fabrics, from plain cottons and satins to pretty prints, or stretch bindings for attaching to stretch knit fabrics. Alternatively, you can make your own (see below).

SINGLE-FOLD BIAS BINDING

The name is a misnomer, as both long edges are folded to the wrong side by about 6 mm (¼ in).

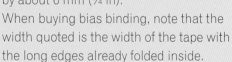

When buying bias binding, note that the width quoted is the width of the tape with the long edges already folded inside.

MAKING YOUR OWN BIAS BINDING

Making your own bias binding means you can match or contrast with your main fabric, giving you more choice of colourways. Check that the binding fabric is compatible with your main fabric in weight and laundering needs.

CALCULATING THE WIDTH OF THE BINDING STRIP

Work out the width of the binding you want to see on the edge of a garment. To achieve a visible width of 1 cm (⅜ in.), which is a nice width in dressmaking, double the visible width required and add 12 mm (½ in.) for seam allowances – so you would need strips 32 mm (1¼ in.) wide. With the long edges turned in by 6 mm (¼ in.) the tape would be 2 cm (¾ in.) and thus 1 cm (⅜ in.) when used and folded over a seam.

CUTTING BIAS STRIPS

Bias-cut strips are used because fabric has more stretch in the bias. The true bias is at a 45-degree angle from the selvedge.

1 To find the true bias, fold the cut edge of the fabric up to one selvedge. The diagonal fold is the bias. Press in a crease and then unfold.

2 Mark your first strip with one edge along the crease. Continue to mark the strips across the fabric to achieve the required length, then cut along the marked lines.

JOINING BIAS STRIPS

To make the required length, place two strips right sides together at right angles to each other at one end. Sew from top left of the joined pieces to bottom right. Trim off the excess, open out and press the seam open. Turn under each long edge of the strip to the wrong side by 6 mm (¼ in.) and press.

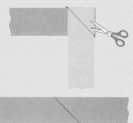

APPLYING BIAS BINDING

To attach binding to cover raw edges, follow these simple steps.

1 Open out one long edge of the bias binding with right sides together, matching the raw edges, pin it to the garment edge. Stitching in the crease of the opened-out fold, machine stitch the binding to the fabric. Trim the seam allowances to 6 mm (¼ in.), clipping and notching curves (see page 44).

2 Fold the binding over the seam allowance to the wrong side, encasing the raw edges, and pin it in place, placing the pins at right angles to the garment edge. Either slipstitch the binding in place by hand or machine stitch from the right side of  the garment, 'stitching in the ditch' by stitching over the first line of stitches, gently pulling the seam apart as you go.

OVERLAPPING ENDS

If the binding ends will meet, the ends will need to be overlapped as inconspicuously as possible.

1 Turn the raw end of the start of the bias binding to the wrong side and press. Pin this end to the garment, 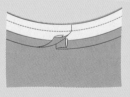 with the long edge unfolded and raw edges even, and follow step 1 above. When you reach the end, allow the unneatened end to overlap the turned start by approximately 1 cm (⅜ in.) and stitch down. When you fold the binding over to the wrong side of the garment, the neatened end will be uppermost.

GOING AROUND CORNERS

You can start each edge separately and then slipstitch the ends together over the edge, or you can fold and turn the binding, which is a neater finish.

1 Mark the seam lines at the corners on the fabric. Stitch the first section of binding to the garment edge as above, ending the stitching where the seams intersect at the corner. Reverse stitch a few stitches, then cut the thread.

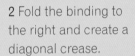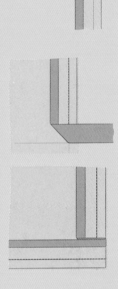

2 Fold the binding to the right and create a diagonal crease.

3 Keeping the crease in place, fold the binding again so that the tape is now along the next edge, ready to be sewn in place.

4 Keeping the folded triangle of tape out of the way, carefully insert the needle into the corner intersection point and continue stitching to the next corner. Repeat for each corner.

5 Turn the binding to the wrong side as before, making a diagonal fold in the corner. Slipstitch in place, stitching the mitred corner as well if desired.

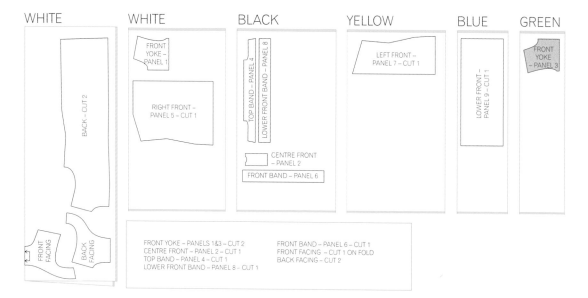

WHITE WHITE BLACK YELLOW BLUE GREEN

BACK – CUT 2

FRONT YOKE – PANEL 1

RIGHT FRONT – PANEL 5 – CUT 1

TOP BAND – PANEL 4

LOWER FRONT BAND – PANEL 8

LEFT FRONT – PANEL 7 – CUT 1

LOWER FRONT – PANEL 9 – CUT 1

FRONT YOKE – PANEL 3

CENTRE FRONT – PANEL 2

FRONT BAND – PANEL 6

FRONT FACING

BACK FACING

FRONT YOKE – PANELS 1&3 – CUT 2
CENTRE FRONT – PANEL 2 – CUT 1
TOP BAND – PANEL 4 – CUT 1
LOWER FRONT BAND – PANEL 8 – CUT 1

FRONT BAND – PANEL 6 – CUT 1
FRONT FACING – CUT 1 ON FOLD
BACK FACING – CUT 2

LAYOUT PLAN Trace off the pattern pieces – front panels 1–9, back, and the front and back facings. After preparing your fabric, fold it as shown on the layout for the width of fabric you are working with. Lay out the pattern pieces as shown. Measure to the selvedge to make sure that the grain is straight. Cut out and transfer any markings to the fabric (see Get Set to Sew, page 21).

2 With right sides together, matching all notches, pin and stitch front panel 4 to the bottom of the yoke section. Press the seam down towards the hem.

1 **MAKE UP THE FRONT OF THE DRESS** With right sides together, matching all notches, pin and stitch panels 1, 2 and 3 together. Press the seams towards the sides. Staystitch (see page 29) the neckline by stitching with a regular 2.5 stitch length 1 cm (⅜ in.) from the edge, sewing from the side edges to the centre. This completes the yoke section.

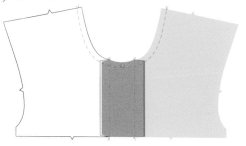

3 With right sides together, matching all notches, pin and stitch front panels 5, 6 and 7 together. Press the seams towards the sides. This completes the mid section of the dress.

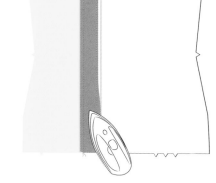

4 With right sides together, matching all notches, pin and stitch front panel 8 to the bottom edge of the mid section, then pin and stitch front panel 9 to the bottom edge of front panel 8. Press the top seam up and the bottom seam down, towards the hem. This completes the lower front section of the dress.

6 SEW THE BACK DARTS
Following the instructions on page 150 and matching the marks from the pattern, fold, pin and sew the double-ended (or fish-eye) darts in the back. Press the darts towards the side seams.

5 With right sides together, pin and stitch the yoke section to the lower front section. Press the seam towards the hem.

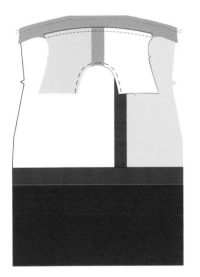

7 STITCH THE FRONT TO THE BACK
With right sides together, pin and stitch the front to the back at the shoulders. Press the seams open.

8 With right sides together, pin and the stitch the front facing to the back facing at the shoulders. Press the seams open. Hem the facing pieces by zigzagging the raw lower edges.

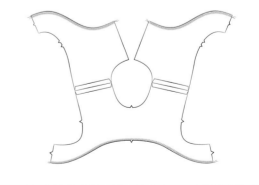

9 ATTACH THE FACING

Lay the dress flat, with the right side facing up. Lay the facing right side down on top, matching up the cut edges of the neckline and the shoulder seams. Pin, then sew around the neckline and armholes. (As the seams are curved, take care to sew slowly.) Clip the seam allowances to allow the curves to sit flat when turned right side out.

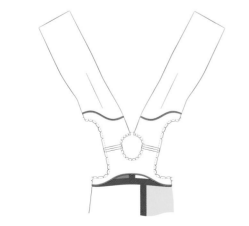

10

Attach a safety pin to one corner of each back piece. Working on one side at a time, use the safety pin to slide the back piece under the facing and through the shoulder seam towards the front of the dress. Repeat on the opposite shoulder.

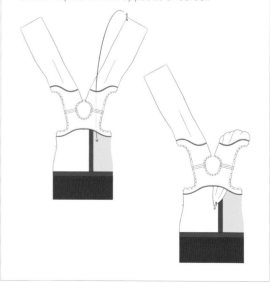

11 From the wrong side, press the facing really flat at the armholes and neckline, rolling the seams towards the wrong side as you press.

12 Neaten the raw edges of the centre back pieces and press. Lay the zip on the dress, with the top of the teeth 1.5cm (⅝ in) from the raw edge, mark the zip stop position in the seam allowance. Remove the zip. With right sides together, pin and stitch the two back pieces, stitching with a long tacking stitch from the neck down to the zip stop mark, then reduce the stitch length to 2.2 and sew the rest of the seam to the hem. Press the back seam open. Following the instructions on page 122, insert the lapped zip.

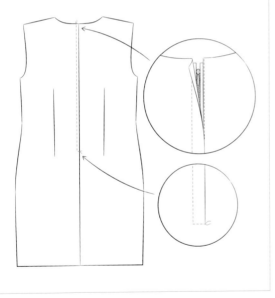

13 With the dress inside out, lift up the facing at the side seam and pin and stitch the side seams from the top of the facing through the underarm seam all the way down to the hem; be sure to match the underarm seams and the hem. Press the seams open and turn the facing to the wrong side of the garment, pressing the armhole edge. Hand stitch the hem of the facing to the seam allowance at the side seams.

14 HEM THE DRESS
Make a double-turned hem by pressing 6 mm (¼ in.) and then 2.5 cm (1 in.) to the wrong side (see page 46). Machine in place close to the inner folded edge.

CORE SKILL
Lining techniques

Adding a lining can improve the way a garment hangs, help it to crease less, prevent bagging at the seat in dresses, skirts and trousers, avoid show-through on transparent fabrics and make it much easier to slip on and off. Lining pieces are generally cut from the same pattern pieces as the main garment, omitting the waistband, collar or facings. There are two methods of insertion: the interlining method, also known as construction lining, and the slip-lining method.

LINING FABRICS

A frequently used fabric for lining is an anti-static polyester. It is lightweight, so it doesn't change the drape of the garment, but it does help with all the things mentioned above as well as preventing static build-up. Although it is available in all sorts of colours, lining fabric doesn't have as much 'give' as most fashion fabrics. Another option is a fine cotton lawn, which has the same properties as other cotton fabrics and comes in a good range of colours; as it is made from natural fibres, it will allow the garment to 'breath' more. A cotton lining is a good option for summer-weight clothing.

Coats and jackets are often lined in a heavier-weight lining or satin to give a rich, full body to the lining. As with the anti-static lining, these can fray easily so it is important to neaten the raw edges.

LINING A SKIRT OR DRESS

Both the Interlining or the Slip Lining methods of lining a skirt can be used on any skirt or dress pattern, even those without linings included in the instructions.

INTERLINING (CONSTRUCTION LINING) METHOD

1 Cut the lining from the same pattern pieces as the skirt, except for the waistband and facing. Transfer marks for centres, notches and darts to the lining fabric, in the same way as for the main fabric (see Get Set to Sew, page 21).

2 With the marked side uppermost, pin the lining to the wrong side of the skirt pieces with raw edges even, matching the centres and notches. Tack together 13 mm (½ in.) from the raw edges and through the centre line of the darts.

3 Make up the skirt, treating the two layers as one, until you are ready to hem.

4 Mark the hem length up from the floor (see Preparing the Hem Allowance, page 46). Then either:

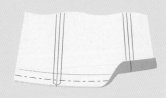

A Unfold the hem. Hand tack the lining to the skirt about 13 mm (½ in.) below the hem fold, with long and short running stitches. Then turn up the hem and finish using your preferred method (see page 46).

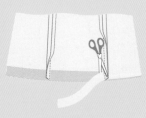

B Unfold the hem. Trim the hem allowance on the lining away along the fold line. Then turn up the skirt hem again and finish using your preferred method (see page 46).

SLIP-LINING METHOD

With this method, the lining and skirt are worked separately and then sewn together at the waistline.

1 Cut the lining from the same pattern pieces as the skirt, excluding the waistband.

2 First, make up the main fabric skirt, except for the waistband and hem.

3 Make up the lining skirt, leaving an opening for the zip 2.5 cm (1 in.) longer than in the skirt. Press the seams open and the waist darts away from the centre.

4 With wrong sides together, matching the darts, centres and side seams and aligning the raw edges at the waistline, pin the lining to the skirt. Turn under the edges of the lining along the zip tape and slipstitch to the tape.

5 Machine baste the waistline edges together 13 mm (½ in.) from the edge. Following the pattern instructions, sew the waistband or facing to the skirt.

6 Hem the skirt first, turning up an equal distance from the floor. Then make the lining hem approximately 13 mm (½ in.) shorter than the skirt. (The lining hem can be a machine-stitched hem.)

LINING A DRESS

1 Follow steps 1 to 4 for slip-lining a skirt, attaching the lining to the dress at armholes and neckline.

FOR A SLEEVELESS DRESS

2 Following the pattern instructions, attach the armhole facings.

FOR A DRESS WITH SLEEVES

2 Following the pattern instructions, attach the main fabric sleeve to the main fabric dress.

3 Sew the sleeve lining underarm seam, press the seam open, and turn right side out. With wrong sides together, matching the markings, pin the sleeve lining to sleeve of the dress. Turn under the seam allowance on the lining sleeve head and hand slipstitch it over the armhole seam.

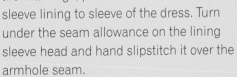

4 Trim the sleeve lining level with the lower edge of the sleeve. Turn under 13 mm (½ in.) on the sleeve lining and slipstitch it over the sleeve hem.

HACK

COLOUR-BLOCKED TOP

This striking two-tone top is a cropped version of the 1960s Colour-Blocked Dress on pages 126–135. Experiment with different colour combinations to suit your personality.

MATERIALS
1.4 m (1½ yd) main fabric, 115 cm (45 in.) wide (for the back, plus front panels 1, 3, 5 and 7)

40 cm (½ yd) contrast fabric, 115 cm (45 in.) wide (for front panels 2, 4 and 6)

25-cm (10-in.) invisible zip

Matching sewing thread

Basic sewing kit (see page 10)

DIFFICULTY LEVEL
Beginner/Intermediate

FABRIC SUGGESTIONS
Light- or medium-weight cottons and cotton blends, cotton sateen, medium-weight double knits like a fine ponte di Roma, crepe de chine, lightweight wool blends, silk shantung, lightweight duchess satin.

DESIGN NOTES
Cut all the front pieces with both the fabric and the pattern piece right side up.

Use a 1.5-cm (⅝-in.) seam allowance throughout, unless otherwise stated.

FINISHED MEASUREMENTS	8	10	12	14	16	18	20
BUST (cm)	88.75	93.75	98.75	103.75	109.75	115.75	121.75
BUST (in.)	34⅞	36⅞	38⅞	40⅞	43¼	45½	47⅞
WAIST (cm)	82.75	87.75	92.75	97.75	103.75	109.75	115.75
WAIST (in.)	32½	34½	36½	38½	40⅞	43¼	45½

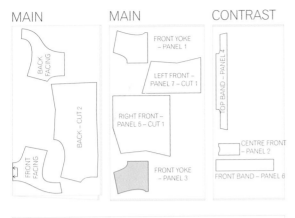

MAIN   MAIN   CONTRAST

BACK FACING

BACK – CUT 2

FRONT FACING

FRONT YOKE – PANEL 1

LEFT FRONT – PANEL 7 – CUT 1

RIGHT FRONT – PANEL 5 – CUT 1

FRONT YOKE – PANEL 3

TOP BAND – PANEL 4

CENTRE FRONT – PANEL 2

FRONT BAND – PANEL 6

FRONT FACING – CUT 1 ON FOLD
BACK FACING – CUT 2
FRONT YOKE – PANELS 1&3 – CUT 2

TOP BAND – PANEL 4 – CUT 1
CENTRE FRONT – PANEL 2 – CUT 1
FRONT BAND – PANEL 6 – CUT 1

LAYOUT PLAN

Trace off the pattern pieces – front panels 1–7, back (following the shorter cutting line marked on the pattern for the back piece and panels 5–7) and the front and back facings. After preparing your fabric, fold it as shown on the layout for the width of fabric you are working with. Lay out the pattern pieces as shown. Measure to the selvedge to make sure that the grain is straight. Cut out and transfer any markings to the fabric (see Get Set to Sew, page 21).

1 MAKE UP THE TOP

Following steps 1–12 of the 1960s Colour-Blocked Dress on page 127, but omitting steps 4 and 6, assemble the top. Following the instructions on page 108, insert a concealed zip at the neck of the centre back seam, then close the seam below the zip.

2 Make a narrow double-turned hem by pressing 1 cm (⅜ in.) and then a second 1 cm (⅜ in.) to the wrong side (see page 46). Machine in place, close to the inner folded edge.

PALAZZO PANTS

PALAZZO PANTS

These simple wide-legged trousers are flattering for any figure and are great for day or evening. The side zip gives a smooth line under tops and the wide leg gives a stunning silhouette – perfect with either flat shoes or heels.

MATERIALS
2.1 m (2¼ yd) fabric, 115 or 150 cm (45 or 60 in.) wide

25 cm (10 in.) fusible interfacing

18-cm (7-in.) concealed zip

Hook and bar fastener

Matching sewing thread

Basic sewing kit (see page 10)

DIFFICULTY LEVEL
Beginner/Intermediate

FABRIC SUGGESTIONS
Cotton, linen, crepe, satin, velvet.

DESIGN NOTES
These wide-legged trousers are cut to sit 4 cm (1½ in.) below the waistline. They have an invisible zip inserted into the side seam and a waistband finished with a hook and eye. The invisible zip is inserted into the left leg side seam before the seam is stitched, thus it is one of the first steps in construction. A regular zip can be used instead, in which case insert it after the rest of the seam is stitched, using the lapped zip insertion method (see page 122).

Use a 1.5-cm (⅝-in.) seam allowance throughout.

FINISHED MEASUREMENTS	8	10	12	14	16	18	20
WAIST (cm)	82	87	92	97	103	109	115
WAIST (in.)	32¼	34½	36¼	38⅛	40½	42⅞	45¼
HIP (cm)	103	108	113	118	124	130	136
HIP (in.)	40½	42½	44½	46½	48¾	51⅛	53½

BACK – CUT 2

FRONT – CUT 2

WAISTBAND – CUT 1 IN FABRIC
AND 1 IN INTERFACING

LAYOUT PLAN

Trace off the pattern pieces – front, back and waistband. After preparing your fabric, fold it in half widthways, right sides together, and lay out the pattern pieces as shown. Measure to the selvedge to make sure that the grain is straight. Cut out and transfer any markings to the fabric (see Get Set to Sew, page 21).

1 Staystitch (see page 29) the upper edge of the front and back pieces 13 mm (½ in.) from the edge, stitching with a regular 2.5 stitch length just inside the seam allowance and stitching from the outer edge to the centre each time.

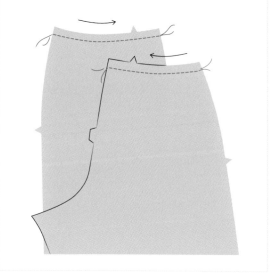

TIP

Neaten the raw edges of the front and back pattern pieces before construction; seams can then be easily pressed open once they have been stitched.

2 STITCH THE DARTS
Fold the waist darts on the back pieces by folding the fabric right sides together, matching the dart markings. Tack and stitch from the top edge, tapering to the fold of the fabric at the tip and taking the last two or three stitches right on the fold. Do not backstitch; instead, leave thread tails and tie off the ends. Press the darts towards the centre back.

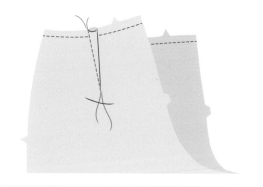

3 INSERT THE INVISIBLE ZIP
Pin the left front and back trouser legs right sides together, matching the notches. Insert the invisible zip into the side seam (see page 108), with the top of the zip teeth 1.5 cm (⅝ in.) from the top of the waist.

4 STITCH THE SIDE AND INSIDE LEG SEAMS

Pin the remaining side seam below the zip. Position the regular zip foot to the left of the foot holder, so that the needle will go down through the outer notch of the foot, and start stitching 6 mm (¼ in.) above the zip stitching and very slightly to the left. Press the seam open.

TIP

Do not try and start stitching right on the zip stitching, as it is almost impossible and can result in a bubble of fabric on the right side.

5

Pin the right front and back trouser legs right sides together, matching the notches, and stitch down the side seam. Press the seam open.

6

Matching the notches, pin and stitch the front to the back at the inside leg seams, stretching the back to fit. Press the seam open. Repeat steps 5 and 6 for the left leg.

7

Turn one leg right side out and slip it inside the other, so the right sides are together, matching the inner leg seams, notches and raw edges. Pin, then stitch the crotch seam, then stitch over the first stitching again to reinforce the seam. Trim the seam allowance and neaten the raw edges. Press the seam open and turn the trousers right side out.

TIP

To reinforce the crotch seam, you could use a triple stretch stitch as an alternative to stitching the seam twice.

8 ATTACH THE WAISTBAND

Trim the interfacing all the way around by 1 cm (⅜ in.) and then centre it on the wrong side of the waistband and fuse it in place. Once cool, turn under the seam allowance on the long, un-notched edge of the waistband. Press and trim the seam allowance to 1 cm (⅜ in.).

9

With right sides together, matching the notches to the seams and the large dots to the waistband opening edges, pin the waistband to the upper edge of the garment. (Note that the front will be longer than the back.) Stitch, trim the seam allowance and press the seam towards the waistband.

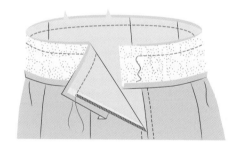

10

With right sides together, fold the waistband in half widthways. Stitch across the short ends and trim the seam allowance.

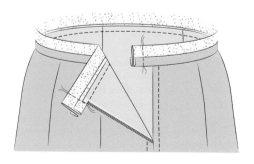

11

Turn the waistband right side out and press, pushing the ends out with a point turner to get a crisp end. Slipstitch the pressed edge over the seam and slipstitch the extension edges together.

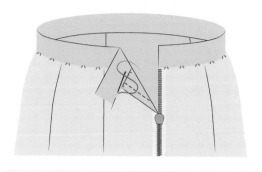

12

Sew a hook and bar fastener to the waistband.

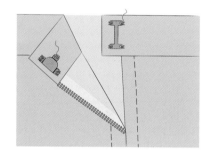

13

Turn up the hem to the correct length and neaten the raw edge. Slipstitch the hem in place, or blind hem by hand or by machine (see page 115).

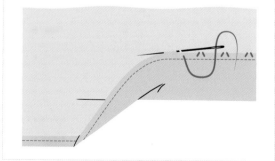

HACK

CULOTTES

Get set for summer by cutting off the Palazzo Pants pattern (page 139) at the marked optional line to make a fashionable pair of culottes. You can also add an in-seam pocket to the right-hand side by following these instructions.

MATERIALS
1.6 m (1¾ yd) fabric, 115 or 150 cm (45 or 60 in.) wide

25 cm (10 in.) fusible interfacing

18-cm (7-in.) concealed zip

Hook and bar fastener

Matching sewing thread

Basic sewing kit (see page 10)

DIFFICULTY LEVEL
Beginner/Intermediate

FABRIC SUGGESTIONS
Cotton, linen, crepe, satin.

DESIGN NOTES
Use a 1.5-cm (⅝-in.) seam allowance throughout.

FINISHED MEASUREMENTS	8	10	12	14	16	18	20
WAIST (cm)	82	87	92	97	103	109	115
WAIST (in.)	32¼	34½	36¼	38⅛	40½	42⅞	45¼
HIP (cm)	103	108	113	118	124	130	136
HIP (in.)	40½	42½	44½	46½	48¾	51⅛	53½

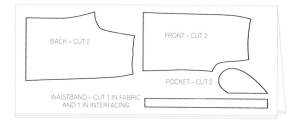

BACK – CUT 2

FRONT – CUT 2

POCKET – CUT 2

WAISTBAND – CUT 1 IN FABRIC
AND 1 IN INTERFACING

LAYOUT PLAN

Trace off the pattern pieces – front, back, waistband and pocket – following the shorter cutting line on the front and back pieces of the Palazzo Pants. After preparing your fabric, fold it in half widthways, right sides together, and lay out the pattern pieces as shown. Measure to the selvedge to make sure that the grain is straight. Cut out and transfer any markings to the fabric (see Get Set to Sew, page 21).

TIP

Cut the pockets in a lightweight lining or cotton lawn fabric rather than fashion fabric, if using a medium weight for the culottes. This will reduce the bulk created by pockets.

If you are 'pear' shaped, leave out the pocket altogether to produce a smoother, slimmer silhouette.

1 Staystitch (see page 29) the upper edge of the front and back pieces 13 mm (½ in.) from the edge, stitching with a regular 2.5 stitch length just inside the seam allowance and stitching from the outer edge to the centre seam each time.

2 On the right leg side seam, mark the position of the top of the pocket 3 cm (1¼ in.) below the top edge.

3 With right sides together, and the straight edge of the pocket along the raw edge of the garment, pin one pocket piece in place. Sew in place along the seam line. Repeat on the back garment section.

4 Press the pocket pieces away from the garment along the stitching. Then place the back and front of the garment right sides together, matching up the pockets. Pin the side seams and the pocket (which extends beyond the garment). Stitch the garment seam, pivoting at the top of the pocket to continue around the pocket bag, and pivoting again to continue down the garment seam.

5 Neaten the raw edges of the pocket with a zigzag or overedge stitch. Snip into the seam allowance at the top and bottom pivot points and press the pocket towards the front of the garment.

6 Make up the culottes, following steps 2–13 of the Palazzo Pants on page 139.

CHINESE-INSPIRED TOP

CHINESE-INSPIRED TOP

The design of this top is based on the qipao – a traditional Chinese dress. The early version of this collarless, tube-shaped gown was worn by both genders in the 17th century. There are many varieties in length, from tops to short dresses and long gowns, with or without sleeves. Its fitted, flattering shape makes it ideal as an evening top or dress.

MATERIALS
1.7 cm (1⅞ yd) fabric, 115 cm (45 in.) wide

50 cm (20 in.) lightweight iron-on interfacing

50 cm (20 in.) ready-made bias binding, 13 mm (½ in.) or 2.5 cm (1 in.) wide

Invisible zip, 25 cm (10 in.) or longer

2 sets of frog fasteners

2 pairs of snap fasteners, 13 mm (½ in.) in diameter

1 hook and eye, size ⅔

Matching sewing thread

Basic sewing kit (see page 10)

DIFFICULTY LEVEL
Intermediate

FABRIC SUGGESTIONS
Medium-weight fabrics such as satin, brocade, faille or challis.

DESIGN NOTES
This is an asymmetric garment, so all front pieces should be cut with both the pattern piece and the fabric facing up.

Use a 1.5-cm (⅝-in.) seam allowance throughout, unless otherwise stated.

FINISHED MEASUREMENTS	8	10	12	14	16	18	20
BUST (cm)	89	94	99	104	110	116	122
BUST (in.)	35	37	39	41	43¼	45⅝	48
WAIST (cm)	70.75	75.75	80.75	85.75	91.75	97.75	103.75
WAIST (in.)	27¾	29¾	31¾	33¾	36	38½	40¾
HIP (cm)	95	100	105	110	116	122	128
HIP (in.)	37⅜	39⅜	41⅜	43¼	45⅝	48	50⅜

CORE SKILL
Darts

Garments are shaped with darts to fit over body contours at bust, hips, through the midriff and at the shoulders. The majority of darts are V-shaped, with the widest part at the outer edge, tapering to a point in the garment. Double darts, which are widest in the middle tapering to a point at either end, are used for waist darts, to provide a closer fit on dresses, fitted jackets and shirts.

SINGLE DARTS

1 Having marked the dart position and length, fold the fabric right sides together, so the marks sit one on top of the other (check by pinning through the layers). Either pin along the stitching line or mark

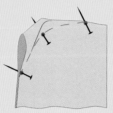

the line with a chalk pencil and then pin at right angles to the dart.

2 Starting at the garment edge, sew towards the point, taking the last two or three stitches in the fold of fabric at the very point. Do not back stitch; either fix/lock stitch, or leave long thread tails and knot the ends together.

3 Press waist darts towards the centre of the garment and press bust darts downwards. Bust darts are added to give shape to the bodice, so they need to be pressed carefully to keep the shaping. To do so, press the dart over a tailor's ham (or a rolled towel, or use the

end of the ironing board), holding the side seam up as you press into the tip.

4 On heavyweight fabrics that would cause a ridge if pressed to one side, cut open the fold of fabric to within 1 cm (⅜ in.) of the tip and press open.

DOUBLE-ENDED DARTS

A double-ended dart can be used to shape the back of the garment from shoulder to hip, or the front from below bust to hip.

1 Fold out the dart, with right sides together, and pin or tack. Start stitching at the centre, stitching to one point, then fix/lock stitch or leave thread tails to knot.

2 Flip the fabric over to stitch the other side, starting at the centre again and slightly overlapping the stitching at the centre by 1 cm (⅜ in.). Stitch to the other point, stitching the last two or three stitches on the fold.

3 To help the dart curve into the body and the folded fabric to lie flat, cut a wedge out of the widest part of the dart fold. On fabrics that fray easily, add a tiny dab of fray check. Press the dart towards the centre front or back of the garment.

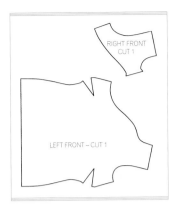

COLLAR – CUT 2 IN FABRIC AND 2 IN INTERFACING
FRONT ARMHOLE FACING – CUT 2 IN FABRIC AND 2 IN INTERFACING
BACK ARMHOLE FACING – CUT 2 IN FABRIC AND 2 IN INTERFACING

LAYOUT PLAN

Trace off the pattern pieces – left front, right front, back, collar and front and back armhole facing pieces. After preparing your fabric, fold one selvedge in to the centre, right sides together, and lay out the pattern pieces as shown, cutting the front pieces from a single layer, with both fabric and pattern right side up so that the pieces don't 'mirror' onto the wrong half of the body. Measure to the selvedge to make sure that the grain is straight. Cut out and transfer any markings to the fabric (see Get Set to Sew, page 21).

1 Staystitch (see page 29) around the necklines and armholes 6 mm (¼ in.) from the edge by stitching with a regular 2.5 stitch length just inside the seam allowance, sewing from the side edges to the centre on the necklines.

2 Neaten the edges of the side seams, shoulder seams and armhole facings, using zigzag stitch or overlocking.

3 INSERT THE DARTS
Fold the bust darts on the left front by folding the fabric right sides together, matching the dart markings. Tack and stitch from the side seam, tapering to the fold of the fabric at the tip and taking the last two or three stitches right on the fold. Do not backstitch; instead, leave thread tails and tie off the ends. Press the bust darts over a ham (see Darts, opposite). Press the darts towards the hem.

4 Following the instructions opposite, fold, pin and sew the double-ended (or fisheye) darts in the back and the left front. Press the darts towards the side seams.

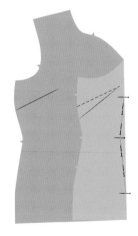

5 HEM THE RIGHT FRONT EDGES
Along the inner edge of the right front panel, press under and pin a 1-cm (⅜-in.) fold. Topstitch in place. Then press under, pin and topstitch a 1-cm (⅜-in.) hem along the bottom edge.

6 BIND THE LEFT FRONT NECKLINE
With right sides together, pin the bias binding along the curved edge of the left front, stopping at the notch. Cut off any excess, leaving a 2-cm (¾-in.) tail at the lower end of the front only. Stitch in place along the pressed crease in the binding.

7
Fold the binding to the wrong side of the garment. Press and pin in place, making sure no binding is visible from the outside.

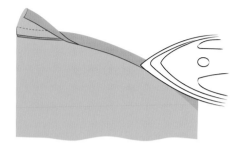

8
With right sides together, pin and sew the two front panels to the back panel at the shoulder seams. Press the seams open.

9 ATTACH THE INVISIBLE ZIP
Following the instructions on page 108, insert the invisible zip into the seam between the back panel and the right-hand edge (as worn) of the left front panel, between the notches. Encase the top of the zip tape in the binding and pin. Topstitch the binding, catching the zip tape within it.

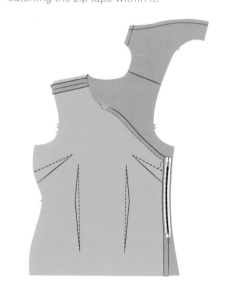

10 With right sides together, lining up the armholes and matching the notches, pin the right front panel to the back along the side seam, above the zip. Stitch down to the notch, making sure you catch the top of the zip tape inside to hide it.

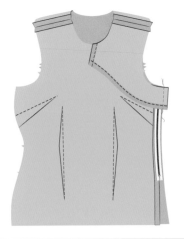

11 Using a regular zip foot, finish stitching the right side seam from the bottom of the zip down to the hem. Press the seam open.

12 With right sides together, lining up the armholes and matching the notches, pin and stitch the left front to the back along the left side seam. Press the seam open.

13 MAKE UP THE COLLAR

Following the manufacturer's instructions, apply iron-on interfacing to the wrong side of the two collar pieces. Turn the bottom edge of the inner collar to the wrong side by 1 cm (⅜ in.) and press. With right sides together, pin and the stitch the two collar pieces together along the curved top edge. Trim the seam allowances to 6 mm (¼ in.), and notch to reduce the bulk inside the seam. Turn the collar right side out and press to create a clean edge.

14

With right sides together, matching the notches, pin the raw edge of the outside collar to the neckline. You'll need to ease the two curves together, so pin carefully. Machine together with a 1-cm (⅜-in.) seam allowance.

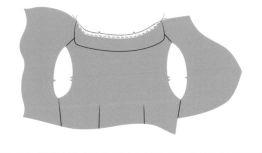

15

Working from the wrong side, press the outside collar seam allowance to the inside of the collar. Line up the pressed fold along the bottom edge of the inner collar, covering the stitch line from the previous step. Pin in place from the right side and topstitch.

16 FINISH OFF THE ARMHOLES

Apply iron-on interfacing to the wrong sides of the front and back armhole facings. With right sides together, pin and stitch a front facing to a back facing along both short ends to form a loop. Repeat with the other front and back facing. Press the seams open. Neaten outer edge of facings with zigzag stitch or overlocking stitch.

17

With right sides together, matching the notches and matching the garment side and shoulder seams to the seams on the facings, pin the facings around the armholes. Machine with a 1-cm (⅜-in.) seam allowance and clip into the seam allowances to make sure you get a flat curve.

18 Open out the facings and press the seam allowances towards the facings and away from the garment. Working from the right side, understitch the facings 3 mm (⅛ in.) away from the seam. This attaches the seam allowance to the facing and stops the edge of the armhole from rolling out.

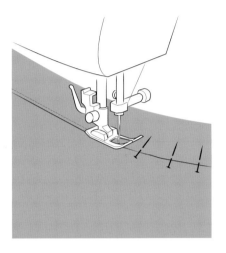

19 Turn the facings inside the armhole and press around the edge, making sure that the seam and understitching are "rolled" towards the inside. Using a simple hand stitch, catch the facings to the seam allowances of the top at the shoulders and the armholes.

20 Around the base of the top, press up a single 1.5-cm (⅝-in.) hem and topstitch in place.

21 Hand stitch popper snaps and frog fasteners to the front opening, with one half on the underside of the left front and the corresponding half on the right side of the right front. Stitch a hook and eye at the neckline, at the base of the collar.

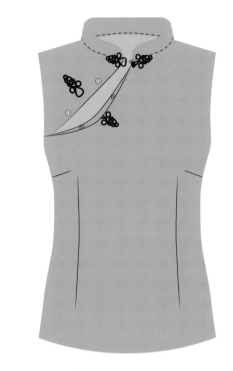

CHAPTER THREE

EXPLORATION

The projects in this chapter combine more challenging techniques with sophisticated fabrics and an exploration of cut and drape. Create a pretty camisole and shorts or bra, a sassy sequin dress or a Japanese-inspired top or cleverly cut skirt. Make a man's sports top or dress shirt, or some dungarees for a toddler. These outfits involve more advanced sewing methods and materials, such as creating pin tucks and sewing with stretch fabrics, but are well worth the effort.

JAPANESE STYLE TOP

JAPANESE-STYLE TOP

This asymmetic draped top is made from only four pieces and is quick and easy to sew. Use a lightweight knit for best results.

MATERIALS
1.5 m (1⅝ yd) stretch knit jersey, 150 cm (60 in.) wide, with a minimum of 30% stretch

Ballpoint needle

Matching sewing thread

Basic sewing kit (see page 10)

DIFFICULTY LEVEL
Intermediate

FABRIC SUGGESTIONS
This top is designed for stretch knit fabrics, such as single or double knits.

DESIGN NOTES
Japanese-style clothes are uniquely cut for unusual drape. Much of the garment can be constructed using an overlocker.

Use a 1.5-cm (⅝-in.) seam allowance throughout, unless otherwise stated.

Check the stretch of your chosen fabric for this project: a 5-cm (2-in.) square should stretch from the grey to white area.

5CM OF FABRIC SHOULD STRETCH FROM HERE   TO AT LEAST HERE ⟶

FINISHED MEASUREMENTS	8	10	12	14	16	18	20
BUST (cm)	99.5	104.5	109.5	114.5	120.5	126.5	132.5
BUST (in.)	39	41	43	45	47½	49¾	52
WAIST (cm)	88.5	93.5	98.5	103.5	109.5	115.5	121.5
WAIST (in.)	34¾	36¾	38¾	40¾	43	45½	47¾
HIP (cm)	87.5	92.5	97.5	102.5	108.5	114.5	120.5
HIP (in.)	34½	36½	38⅛	40⅛	42¾	45	47½

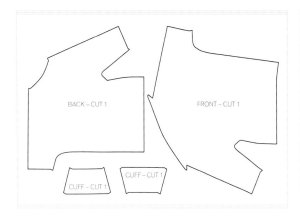

LAYOUT PLAN

Trace off the pattern pieces – front, back and cuff. After preparing your fabric, lay it out as a single layer, with the right side facing up. Lay out the pattern pieces as shown, with the grainlines parallel to the selvedges, and cut out. Transfer any markings to the fabric (see Get Set to Sew, page 21).

2 CONSTRUCT THE TOP

With right sides together, matching the raw edges of the sleeves and hem, pin and then zigzag stitch or overlock the side seams from the hem to the sleeve end. Note that the centre front neck edge extends beyond the back.

1 NEATEN THE NECKLINE EDGES

Turn the centre back neckline over to the wrong side by 6 mm (¼ in.) and then by 6 mm (¼ in.) again, pin in place and zigzag stitch to secure. Neaten the centre front neckline by zigzag stitching or overlocking.

3

Fold the seam allowance of the centre front neckline to the wrong side in line with the back shoulder point. Pin in place, pinning the rest of the shoulder seam as well. Zigzag or overlock the seams.

4 MAKE THE CUFFS

Fold the cuff piece in half, right sides together. Pin and zigzag stitch or overlock the underarm (side) seam. Repeat for the second cuff.

5

With right sides together, aligning the raw edges and matching the underarm seam on the top to the cuff seam, pin the narrower end of the cuffs to the sleeves. Zigzag stitch or overlock.

6

Turn down the cuff. Turn under and pin a 1.5-cm (⅝-in.) hem on both the top and the cuffs and secure with a zigzag stitch. Press and the top is finished.

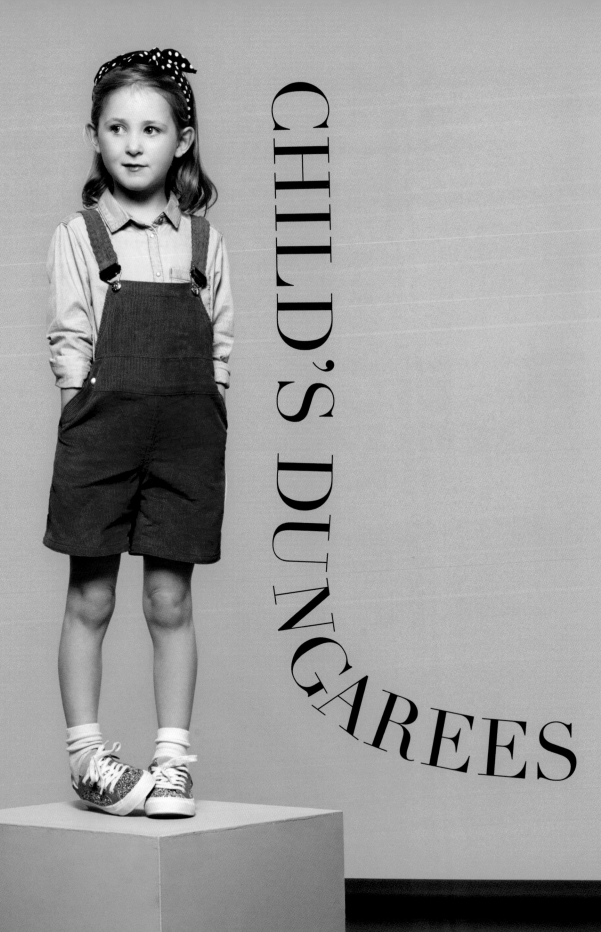

CHILD'S DUNGAREES

CHILD'S DUNGAREES

Make your little tot a pair of sturdy dungarees just like the contestants did in series 2 of *The Great British Sewing Bee*. This is a classic child's garment that never goes out of fashion and looks as cute on girls as it does on boys.

MATERIALS
1 m (1 yd) cotton corduroy, 115 or 150 cm (45 or 60 in.) wide

2 anorak snap fasteners

1 set dungaree clips

2 dungaree buttons

Basic sewing kit (see page 10)

DIFFICULTY LEVEL
Intermediate

FABRIC SUGGESTIONS
Make these in a medium-weight cotton for summer or twill, corduroy or denim for winter.

DESIGN NOTES
These dungarees are fastened with anorak snaps at the sides. Double topstitching has been used to finish and add sturdiness to the seams.

Use a 1.5-cm (⅝-in.) seam allowance throughout, unless otherwise stated.

AGE in years	1	2	3	4
CHEST (cm)	60.5	62.5	64.5	66.5
CHEST (in.)	23¾	24½	25⅛	26⅛
WAIST (cm)	62	64	66	68
WAIST (in.)	24⅛	25⅛	26	26¾

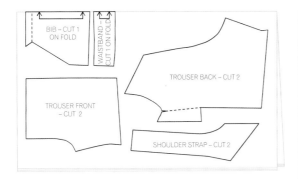

LAYOUT PLAN

Trace off the pattern pieces – trouser front, trouser back, waistband, bib and shoulder strap. After preparing your fabric, fold it as shown on the layout and lay out the pattern pieces, making sure that all pieces are facing the same direction if you are using a pile fabric (so that the pile brushes downwards). Measure to the selvedge to make sure that the grain is straight. Cut out and transfer any markings to the fabric (see Get Set to Sew, page 21).

1 With right sides together, pin and stitch the trouser fronts together at the centre front seam. Press the seam allowances towards the right front, then double topstitch the seam from the right side.

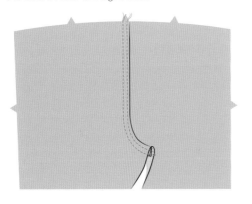

2 Along the un-notched edge of the waistband, press under a 1.5-cm (⅝-in.) fold to the wrong side. With right sides together, pin the waistband to the trouser front. Tack in place 6 mm (¼ in.) from the edge.

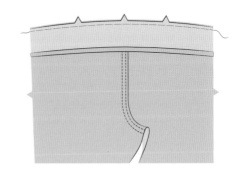

3 Pin the bib and trouser front wrong sides together, so that the trouser front is sandwiched between the bib and the waistband. Stitch together.

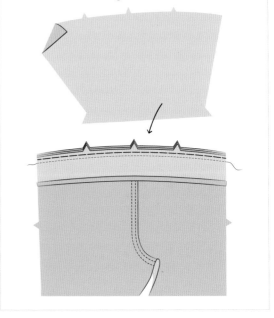

4 Press the seams open at the front, then press the waistband piece upwards. Working from the right side, double topstitch the waistband.

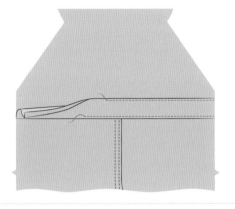

5 Attach a shoulder strap to each trouser back, using flat fell seams (see page 42).

6 On the back piece, fold the facing over so that it's right sides together and level with the underarm edge, and press. Stitch across the width of the facing 2 cm (¾ in.) from the top edge. Turn the facing to the wrong side of the back and press. Repeat for the other back piece.

7 Turn under 2 cm (¾ in.) along both long edges of the shoulder straps, then fold under the raw edges. Double topstitch each strap from the right side. Zigzag the raw short ends.

8 With right sides together, matching the strap seams, stitch the backs together. Zigzag the seam allowances together, then press the seam allowance towards the left back. Double topstitch the seam from the right side.

9 With right sides together, matching the dots, notches and bottom edges, pin the front to the back along the outside leg seams. Stitch from the bottom up to the dot. Zigzag the seam allowances together.

10 On the top edge of the bib, fold the facing over so that it is right sides together and level with the main part of the bib and press. Stitch each short side of the facing, 2 cm (¾ in.) from the edge. Turn the facing to the wrong side of the bib and press.

CORE SKILL
Snap fasteners

Snap fasteners can add a really pretty and professional finish to garments, particularly children's clothing. They come in different sizes and colours. Many also come with a set of tools for handy application, and instructions for use on the back of the pack.

TIPS

Try out the snap on a scrap of the fabric, with the same layers and interfacing. Work on a solid surface, such as the floor, protected by a block of wood such as a chopping board.

ATTACHING LIGHTWEIGHT SNAPS

1 Snaps are made up of four parts, two for each half of the snap. On lightweight snaps there are two washers with prongs that are pushed through the fabric and then the snap top with the nub and the snap bottom with the recess into which the nub fits. Start by pairing up the pieces.

2 Line up the two garment pieces where the snap is to go and push a pin through both layers. Using a marking pen, mark the snap positions.

3 Push the prongs of one washer through from the underside to the right side of the

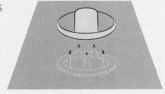

lower section of fabric. Then insert the top of the snap with the centre nub right side up over the prongs. Cover with the tool and hammer together to spread the prongs and hold the first half of the snap in place.

4 Fix the second half of the snap by pushing the prongs of the front of the snap through from the right side to the underside of the lapping section. Having the underside of the lapped section uppermost, drop on the washer, with the ridge down towards the fabric. Cover with the tool and hammer the snap pieces together.

ATTACHING HEAVYWEIGHT SNAPS

1 For heavy-duty snaps, there are two sockets instead of pronged washers – so you need to make holes in the fabric before the snaps can be applied. Pair up the pieces, as above, so that you have one socket with the smooth snap top (which has a long centre rod), and the lower half of the pairing with a long centre rod to be topped by a larger socket.

2 Mark the snap position on both sections of the garment and then, using the hole punch tool that comes with the snap kit, make a hole at the marked positions. Push the protruding parts through the holes and top with the snap sections, using the tool to protect them and hammering the parts together on each of the garment sections.

11 On the sides of the bib and the side openings, turn under 2 cm (¾ in.), then fold under the raw edges. Double topstitch the side and top edges of the bib from the right side.

13 With right sides together, pin and stitch the inside leg seams. Press the seams open.

14 To hem the legs, fold under 2.5 cm (1 in.) to the wrong side and press. Fold under the raw edges and press. Double topstitch.

12 Press the outside leg seam allowances towards the front. Fold the back facing along the fold line and pin it over the outside leg seam. Double topstitch from the bottom edge of the leg to the topstitching on the side opening. Bar tack between the topstitching at the bottom of the side openings.

15 Following the manufacturer's instructions, attach an anorak snap to each side opening at the waistband. Slide dungaree clips onto the straps and stitch them in place. Attach dungaree buttons to the corners of the bib, snapping them into position with your fingers.

MEN'S CYCLE TOP

MEN'S CYCLE TOP

This bright top, made in a highly stretchy fabric, is both comfortable to wear and practical when exercising. Make it for lounging at the weekends or as active sportswear. It's a quick make when sewn with an overlocker, although you can, of course, use a sewing machine.

MATERIALS
1.6 m (1¾ yd) stretch fabric 150 cm (60 in.) wide, with a minimum of 40% stretch

30 cm (12 in.) knit interfacing

Stretch needle

Matching sewing thread

Basic sewing kit (see page 10)

DIFFICULTY LEVEL
Intermediate

FABRIC SUGGESTIONS
Two- or four-way stretch fabrics with Lycra or spandex. Lycra is a synthetic fibre known for its elasticity, making it ideal for sportswear. Fabrics with a high percentage of Lycra can stretch up to five times their length.

DESIGN NOTES
We have used an overlocker to sew most of this top, but you can make it with a narrow zigzag stitch on a regular sewing machine. Test the best stitch width/length and stitch type on some scrap fabric first, as fabrics with Lycra as part of their composition will sew differently depending on the amount of Lycra included. We've also inserted a short zip, with exposed teeth. Behind the zip is a placket to protect the skin when exercising.

Use a 1-cm (⅜-in.) seam allowance throughout, unless otherwise stated.

Check the stretch of your fabric for this project: a 5-cm (2-in.) square should stretch from the grey to white area.

5CM OF FABRIC SHOULD STRETCH FROM HERE   TO AT LEAST HERE →

FINISHED MEASUREMENTS	36	38	40	42	44	46	48
CHEST (cm)	104	107	110.5	113.5	116.75	120	123
CHEST (in.)	41	42¼	43½	44¾	46	47¼	48½
WAIST (cm)	105	108.5	11.75	115	118	121.25	124.5
WAIST (in.)	41½	42¾	44	45¼	46½	47¾	49
HIP (cm)	110.5	113.5	116.75	120	123.75	127	129.5
HIP (in.)	43½	44¾	46	47¼	48¾	50	51

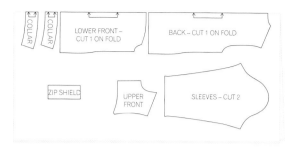

LAYOUT PLAN

Trace off the pattern pieces – upper front, lower front, back, sleeve, collar and zip shield. Lay out the pattern pieces as shown and measure to the selvedge to make sure that the grain is straight. Cut out and transfer any markings to the fabric (see Get Set to Sew, page 21).

1 Fuse 1.25-cm (½-in.) strips of knit interfacing to the wrong side of the zip-placement area on the upper front pieces and front of collar.

2 With right sides together, sew the upper fronts to the back at the shoulders.

3 Open the pieces out so that the neckline edge is one layer at the top. With right sides together, sew one of the collar pieces around the neckline. Fold the collar up and away from the body of the shirt.

4 Prepare the under collar piece by overlocking the lower edge. Set to one side.

5 If you are using an overlocker, switch to a regular sewing machine for the zip insertion. Turn the top right side out. Pin the zip right side down to the upper front pieces and collar, aligning the edge of the tape with the edges of the upper front pieces, placing the bottom zip stop 13 mm (½ in.) above the lower edge, so it doesn't get caught in the overlocker later. Stitch one side of the zip tape to the interfaced edge of one upper front piece, using a straight stitch. Repeat to attach the other side of the zip to the other upper front piece, matching the neckline across the zip.

6 Open the zip. With right sides together, matching the notches, pin the under collar to the top edge of the outer collar and stitch.

7 Press the under collar up, away from the outer collar. Understitch the under collar to the seam allowance along the edge, stitching close to the previous seam.

8 Turn the under collar down, so that the under and outer collars are right sides together. Pin and then sew the short sides of the collar together, using a zipper foot and a straight stitch and taking care not to sew through the zip teeth.

9 Turn the collar right side out. Working from the outside of the garment, pin the under collar so that it sits just over the seam between the collar and the upper fronts and back. Stitch in the ditch along the seamline.

TIP

When working with very stretchy fabric, it is often better to cut each piece from a single layer. Cut all notches outwards (not into the seam allowance). When two pieces are needed, remember to flip the pattern piece over to cut a right- and a left-hand piece.

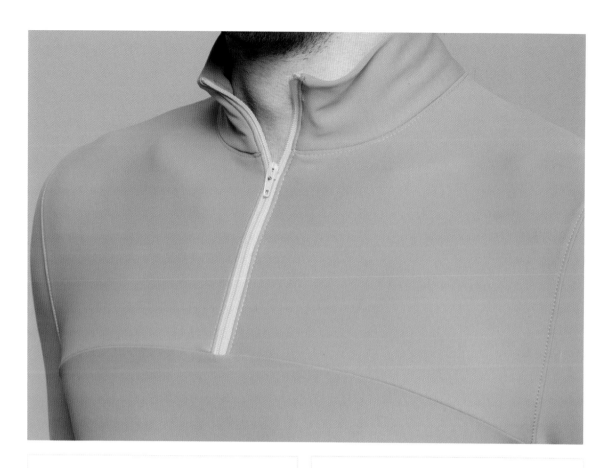

10 Switch back to your overlocker, if you are using one. Fold the zip shield in half lengthways, right sides together, and stitch along one of the raw short edges. Turn right side out and overlock the long raw edges together.

11 Switch back to a regular sewing machine for this step. Place the zip shield behind the zip tape on the right upper front (as worn), aligning the short folded edge of the zip shield with the top edge of the collar and protruding 1 cm (⅜ in.) beyond the zip teeth. Using a zipper foot or a walking foot, stitch close to the edge of the zip through all layers, including the zip shield. Then topstitch close to the zip on the left side, taking care not to catch the zip shield. Close the zip.

12 Switch back to your overlocker, if using. With right sides together, pin and stitch the lower front to the upper front pieces, catching the zip shield and the ends of the zip tape but not the zip stop or the zip teeth.

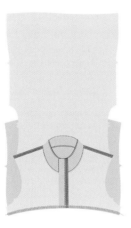

14 Fold the garment in half, right sides together, aligning the underarm seams, waist notches and body panel seams. Sew from sleeve hem to garment hem in one step. Repeat for the other side.

15 Fold under 2 cm (¾ in.) to the inside of the sleeve edge and stitch 2 cm (¾ in.) from the right side, using a twin needle (see page Twin Needle Topstitched Hem, page 47). Hem the bottom of the garment in the same way.

13 Lay out the top right side up, so that the armholes form smooth curves. Ascertain which is the correct sleeve for each armhole curve by checking the notches (matching singles to singles and doubles to doubles). With right sides together, matching the central sleeve head notch with the shoulder seam, position one of the sleeves on top of the corresponding armhole curve. Pin together. Next, match the single notch on the sleeve head with the single notch on the armhole curve and pin together. Do the same with the double notches. Finally, match the underarm points of the sleeve with the beginning and end points of the armhole curve and pin. Stitch the sleeve to the front and back from side seam to side seam. Repeat for the other sleeve.

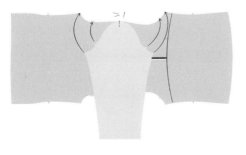

SOFT-CUP BRA

Making your own bra can be the key to getting one to fit perfectly. Using soft lace, power nets and pretty lace trims, you can make a bra that looks beautiful, feels comfortable and is just a fraction of the cost to buy. Our bra pattern is for a soft-cup bra without underwires. Once you have made and fitted one, you can make many more.

MATERIALS
25 cm (10 in.) stretch lace with a minimum of 5% stretch.

25 cm (10 in.) stretch powermesh

32 cm (12½ in.) clear elastic, 4 mm (⅛ in.) wide

124 cm (49 in.) picot-edge plush-back lingerie elastic, 10 mm (⅜ in.) wide

Picot-edge plush-back lingerie elastic, 15 mm (⅝ in.) wide

Pre-made bra hook-and-eye closure, 2 hooks wide, 2.8 cm (1⅛ in.) wide

118 cm (46½ in.) bra strap elastic, 10mm (⅜ in.) wide

2 x O rings and 2 x sliders, 10 mm or 13 mm (⅜ in. or ½ in.) wide

Matching sewing thread

Stretch or microtex needle

Basic sewing kit (see page 10)

DIFFICULTY LEVEL
Intermediate

DESIGN NOTES
We have used a stretch lace and plush-back elastic here. Stretch lace doesn't need to have the edges neatened, because it will not fray.

Use a 6-mm (¼-in.) seam allowance throughout, unless otherwise stated. Check the stretch of your fabric for this project: a 5-cm (2-in.) square should stretch from the grey to white area.

5CM OF FABRIC SHOULD STRETCH   TO AT LEAST HERE →

TO FIT	8	10	12	14	16	18	20
BUST (cm)	83	88	93	98	104	110	116
BUST (in.)	32½	34½	36½	38½	41	43¼	45½

CORE SKILL
Sewing with stretch fabrics

Stretch fabrics are wonderful to wear, and so forgiving to fit as they will stretch over our bodies easily. In order to ensure that any garment you make continues to stretch as it should, it is important to follow a few rules when sewing jersey fabrics.

TYPES OF STRETCH FABRIC

There are different types of stretch fabrics, including lightweight single, medium- and heavyweight double knits, jersey and stretch velour. In addition, Lycra and spandex are two- or four-way stretch fabrics used for sportswear that is tight fitting and requires plenty of stretch.

NEEDLES

Use a ballpoint or stretch needle when sewing with stretch fabrics. A two-way stretch fabric such as Lycra needs a stretch needle, while most jersey fabrics are best sewn with a ballpoint needle. Both these specialist needles, available in different thicknesses for the different weights of knit fabric, have slightly rounded tips to part the fibres rather than pierce them. Using a universal needle can cause skipped stitches.

Use a new needle with each project, as a blunt needle can also snag the fabric. In knits, this can cause runs.

For topstitched hems, consider a ballpoint twin needle, which will sew two perfectly parallel rows on the top and a zigzag stitch on the underside as the bobbin thread switches between the two top threads.

KNIT FABRIC SEAMS

Stretchy fabrics usually still need to stretch, so they need to have flexible seams – particularly seams that go around the body. Stitching with a straight stitch can result in broken stitches when the garment is pulled on and off. To stitch a flexible seam, choose a stretch stitch (above left – it looks like a continuous bolt of lightening) or a small zigzag stitch (above right), reduced to 2.5 width, stretching the fabric slightly as you sew.

FINISHING THE SEAM ALLOWANCE

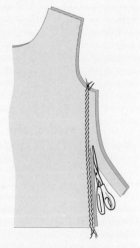

While most knit fabrics do not fray or unravel, the edges can have a tendency to curl, causing bulky seams. To avoid this, stitch with a double seam, which also provides a stronger seam, particularly important for exercise wear. It is formed by stitching two parallel rows close together, working both in the same direction. Stitch the first row, using a stretch stitch or zigzag stitch as above. Stitch again in the seam allowance a scant 3mm (⅛ in.) away, using either a straight or small zigzag stitch, and then trim close to the stitching. Press to set the stitching.

STABILISING SEAMS

There are some areas on a stretch knit garment where the fabric shouldn't stretch too much or they will pull out of shape, such as necklines, shoulder seams and armholes. Avoid unwanted stretch by adding a strip of fusible stabiliser tape (ease tape) to the seam allowance. Alternatively, with right sides together, place seam binding, ribbon or twill tape over the seamline and stitch in place when you stitch the seam.

BIAS SEAMS

Bias-cut fabric will stretch more easily because there is more give on the bias and on stretch fabrics this is even more so. To prevent unwanted stretch and to stop seams rippling, hold the fabric in front and behind of the presser foot, stretching it slightly as you stitch. The stitching will then relax into a smooth seam once carefully pressed to embed the stitching.

Always hang a garment with bias-cut seams for at least 24 hours before hemming to allow the seams to relax and droop (see Hemming, page 46).

DIFFERENT SEAM OPTIONS

As well as sewing a regular seam with a stretch stitch, other useful seams for knit fabrics include lapped seams and flat fell seams (see Seams and Seam Finishes, pages 42–43). Note that horizontal seams are lapped downwards and vertical seams away from the centre.

WELT OR DOUBLE WELT SEAM

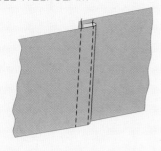

Another useful seam for heavyweight fabrics where bulk can be a problem is a welt or double welt seam. This is also a good method of strengthening the seam and neatening the seam allowances.

1 Stitch a regular seam and press both seam allowances to one side.

2 Grade the seam allowances by trimming the under edge to 6 mm (¼ in.) and leaving the upper seam allowance untrimmed.

3 Working from the right side, topstitch 1 cm (⅜ in.) from the seam, catching the untrimmed seam allowance as you go.

4 To make a double welt seam, add an additional row of edge stitching close to the seamline.

TIP

On very thick fabrics, press the seam allowances open and then topstitch from the right side 1 cm (⅜ in.) from the seam on either side to hold the seam allowances down.

LACE   POWERMESH

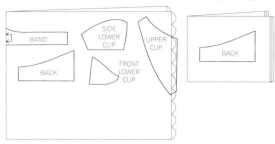

UPPER CUP – CUT 1 PAIR IN MAIN FABRIC
SIDE LOWER CUP – CUT 1 PAIR IN MAIN FABRIC
FRONT LOWER CUP – CUT 1 PAIR IN MAIN FABRIC
BACK – CUT 1 PAIR IN MAIN FABRIC, 1 PAIR IN POWERMESH
BOTTOM BAND – CUT 1 IN MAIN FABRIC

LAYOUT PLAN

Trace off the pattern pieces – upper cup, side lower cup, front lower cup, back panel and bottom band. Arrange the panels on the lace. If your lace has a scallop edge, line the top edge of the upper cup piece along it. Cut all the other panels so that the greatest stretch goes around the body. Allow more fabric for matching of patterns, stripes or fabrics with nap or shine.

TIP

As the seam allowances are only 6 mm (¼ in.), cut pattern marks like notches outwards or simply keep your pattern pieces close by to refer to instead.

1 With right sides together, sew a front lower cup to a side lower cup, then sew an upper cup to the lower-cup section. Repeat for the other side.

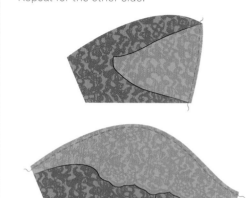

2 Cut your elastic in half. Using a 3-step zigzag stitch, attach clear elastic to the underside of the scallop-edged lace on the upper cup panels. The clear elastic should sit just under the scallop edge. Do not overstretch the elastic: it should be sewn with tension in it, but not super stretched.

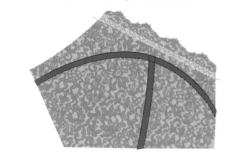

3 With right sides together, sewing from one side to the other and pivoting at the centre, sew on the bottom band.

4 Prepare the back panels by laying the lace pieces on top of the powermesh pieces and machine basting or hand tacking around the outside edges, 6 mm (¼ in.) from the edge. This is a technique called mounting or interlining. The double-layered pieces will be used as single layer from now on.

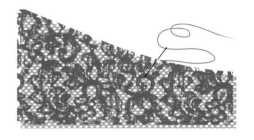

5 With right sides together, attach the back panels to the front at the side seams.

6 Cut two pieces of narrow picot-edge lingerie elastic to the size of the top edge of the bra from the back panel to the top of the upper cup minus 5%. With the elastic right side up on the right side of the bra, pin it in place. Using a straight stitch, sew along the lower picot edge of the elastic. The elastic should be sewn in under tension with a minimal amount of stretch.

7 Turn the elastic to the inside of the bra and pin in place. Using a 3-step zigzag stitch, topstitch the elastic down close to the picot edge. Repeat steps 6 and 7 on the other side of the bra.

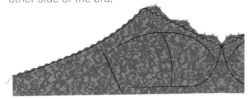

8 Cut a piece of wide picot-edge lingerie elastic to the length of the lower edge of the bra minus 5%. With the elastic right side up on the right side of the bra, pin it in place (overlapping by the seam allowance). Using a straight stitch, sew along the picot edge of the elastic. As before, sew it under tension with a minimal amount of stretch.

9 Turn the elastic to the inside of the bra and pin it in place. Using a 3-step zigzag stitch, topstitch the elastic down, as in step 7.

10 Now attach the hook-and-eye bra fastener to the back of the bra. The eyes are attached facing right side up to the left side of the bra. Insert the edge of the left bra back band into the slit opening on the eye section of the fastener. Topstitch it in place, using a narrow zigzag stitch. The hooks are attached facing right side down onto the right side of the bra. Insert the edge of the right bra back band into the slit opening on the hook section of the fastener, making sure that the hooks are facing downwards. Topstitch in place, using a narrow zigzag stitch.

11 Cut two 55-cm (21½ in.) lengths of bra-strap elastic for the straps, and two 4-cm (1½-in.) lengths for the O ring holders. Take one of the small lengths, slip the O ring on and fold the elastic in half. Place the cut ends of the elastic vertically at the top of the front cups, where the picot elastic meets the clear elastic, with the O ring at the top. Topstitch the elastic in place. Repeat on the other side.

12 Take a long length of elastic and a slider. Feed one end of the elastic through the slider so that it is looped around the central post. Topstitch it in place. Take the opposite end of the same length of elastic and feed it through one of the O rings. Bring it up and feed it back through the slider. Go from underneath, up and over the central post, back down and under the other side to create an adjustable strap. Repeat for the second strap.

12 On the wrong side of the back panel, measure 7 cm (2¾ in.) out from the hook-and-eye closures, fold under the raw edge of the strap and topstitch it in place at both the lower edge and the upper edge of the band, as illustrated. Repeat on the other side.

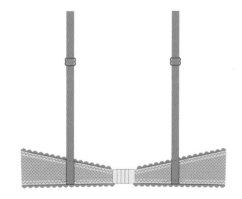

ASYMMETRIC SKIRT

ASYMMETRIC SKIRT

Bunka, the famed fashion school in Japan, has influenced and transformed Western fashion in the last few years. Their clever patterns create unusual shapes and silhouettes that require the maker to truly understand the construction of clothes. This skirt looks like a puzzle when all the pieces are laid flat, but the complex geometric shapes of the flat pieces combine to make an interesting, contemporary skirt.

MATERIALS
2 m (2¼ yd) fabric, 150 cm (60 in.) wide

1–1.5 m (1–1½ yd) grosgrain ribbon, 5 cm (2 in.) wide

Matching sewing thread

Basic sewing kit (see page 10)

DIFFICULTY LEVEL
Intermediate

FABRIC SUGGESTIONS
This skirt has been designed for fabrics with inherent structure that don't fray like boiled wool, double knit jersey, neoprene, scuba or felt.

DESIGN NOTES
This skirt has an asymmetric yoke made from three panels, with a waved lower seamline. The skirt, also constructed from three panels, has no distinct left or right, and could almost be worn in any position on the body. Due to the asymmetrical line between the yoke and the skirt, each panel is cut once only. Construct the yoke and the skirt separately before joining them together with an edge stitch. When attaching the yoke to the skirt, it is very important to match all of the balance marks along the seam. There are 17 in total.

Use a 1.5-cm (⅝-in.) seam allowance throughout, except along the wavy yoke edge, which has a 1-cm (⅜-in.) seam allowance.

FINISHED MEASUREMENTS	8	10	12	14	16	18	20
WAIST (cm)	68.75	73.75	78.75	83.75	89.75	95.75	101.75
WAIST (in.)	27	29	31	33	35¼	37½	40

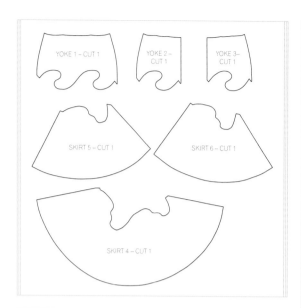

LAYOUT PLAN

Trace off the pattern pieces – 1–3 for the yoke, and 4–6 for the skirt. After preparing your fabric, lay out the pattern pieces face up, as shown. Measure to the selvedge to make sure that the grain is straight. Cut out and transfer any markings to the fabric (see Get Set to Sew, page 21); do not snip any notches along the yoke edge – instead, mark or tack them. (You can, however, snip notches along the side seams.)

1. If desired, neaten the raw edges of the sides and centre back of yoke pieces 1, 2 and 3 and the sides, centre back and hem of skirt pieces 4, 5 and 6 with an overlocker, or an overlock-style or stitch on a sewing machine, thus leaving the wavy edge un-neatened. This is not essential on a fabric that doesn't fray.

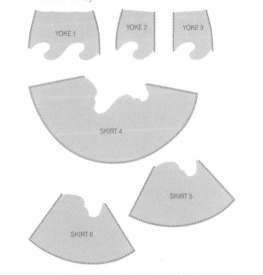

2. With right sides together, matching the notches, sew yoke pieces 1, 2 and 3 together. Press the seam allowances open. This completes the yoke. Mark the seam allowance along the bottom edge of the yoke section by tacking 1 cm (⅜ in.) from the edge.

3 Following the instructions on page 150, fold, pin and stitch the waistline darts in the yoke. Press the darts towards the zip.

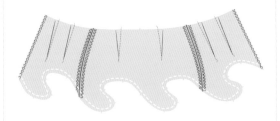

4 With right sides together, matching the notches, sew skirt pieces 4, 5 and 6 together. Press the seam allowances open. This completes the skirt.

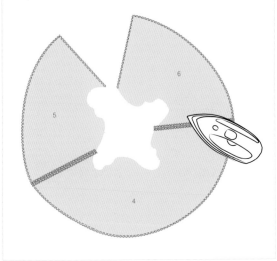

5 With both pieces right side up, lay the yoke on top of the skirt, matching the seam allowance on the upper edge of the skirt to the line tacked in step 2. Match all the balance marks, then pin and tack the two layers together. Clip into the seam allowance on the inside on the skirt only, to release the tension along the inverted curves.

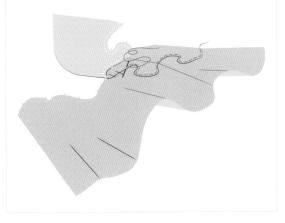

6 Lengthen your stitches to 3 mm (⅛ in.). Working from the right side, topstitch the yoke to the skirt along the previous row of tacking.

7 Following the instructions on page 108, insert a concealed zip in the centre back seam. With right sides together, pin and stitch the rest of the centre back seam, below the zip. Press the seam open.

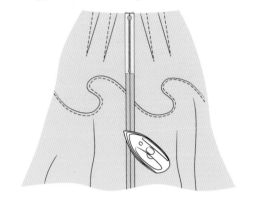

8 Turn up the hem allowance and pin or tack in place. Topstitch to secure. This is not essential on fabric that doesn't fray.

9 Cut a strip of grosgrain ribbon long enough to go around the waist plus 3 cm (1¼ in.). With right sides together, leaving 1.5 cm (⅝ in.) overhanging at each side of the centre back, above the zip, pin and stitch the grosgrain to the waistline of the completed skirt.

10 Press the grosgrain and the seam allowance away from the skirt and then understitch along the grosgrain ribbon close to the previous seam, catching the seam allowance of the skirt as you stitch. Wrap the short ends of the grosgrain around the seam allowance at the centre back, press and then turn the grosgrain ribbon to the inside. Hand stitch the grosgrain to the top of the zip tape and at the side seams to hold it in place.

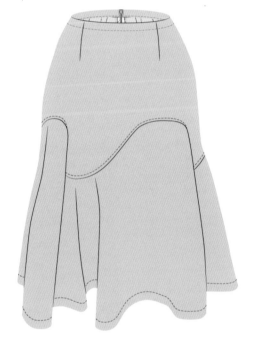

SEQUIN COCKTAIL DRESS

SEQUIN COCKTAIL DRESS

A sequin dress says 'special occasion' more than any other fabric and will be your go-to party dress. The shimmering, shining fabric is the main focus, so the actual dress design can be ultra simple. Just let the fabric do the talking…

MATERIALS

1.5–2 m (1⅝ yd–2¼ yd) sequin jersey fabric 150 cm (60 in.) wide or 2.5–3 m (2¾–3¼ yd) fabric 115 cm (45 in.) wide, with at least 5 per cent elastane

1.5–2 m (1⅝ yd–2¼ yd) stretch jersey 150 cm (60 in.) wide or 2.5–3 m (2¾–3¼ yd) fabric 115 cm (45 in.) wide for lining

1 m (1 yd) power net

1.5 m (1⅝ yd) bias binding, 2 cm (¾ in.) wide and 1 m (1 yd) bias binding, 2.5 cm (1 in.) wide

1 x 1-cm (⅜-in.) ball button

Universal sewing machine needle, size 80/12 and ballpoint or stretch needle, size 80/12

Basic sewing kit (see page 10)

DIFFICULTY LEVEL

Intermediate

FABRIC SUGGESTIONS

Look for soft sequins that can be cut and sewn through, attached to a stretch-fabric base.

DESIGN NOTES

Narrow seams have been used on the net to minimise show-through and the neck and arms are finished with bias binding. Use 1-cm (⅜-in.) seam allowances throughout.

Check the stretch of your fabric for this project: a 5-cm (2-in.) square should stretch from the grey to white area.

5CM OF FABRIC SHOULD STRETCH   TO AT LEAST HERE →

FINISHED MEASUREMENTS	8	10	12	14	16	18	20
BUST (cm)	82	87	92	97	103	109	115
BUST (in.)	32¼	34¼	36¼	38¼	40½	42¾	45¼
WAIST (cm)	65.5	70.5	75.5	80.5	86.5	92.5	98.5
WAIST (in.)	25¾	27¾	29¾	31¾	34	36½	38¾
HIP (cm)	89	94	99	104	110	116	122
HIP (in.)	35	37	39	41	43¼	45½	48

CORE SKILL
Sewing with Sequinned Fabrics

Follow the 'with nap' layouts, making sure that all pieces are laid head to toe in the same direction so that any pile or pattern will be the same on every piece.

Cut from a single layer of fabric with the fabric right side up, remembering to flip the pattern piece over if you need to cut two in order to get a left- and a right-hand side.

Use sew-in interfacings, or use a transparent organza so that it doesn't change the look or handle of the garment.

Make up the garment as a toile/test garment, in a fabric that is similar to your fashion fabric to check fit and finish.

When handling the cut pieces, if the sequins or beads are dropping from the edges, apply drafting tape to the cut edge temporarily until the seams are stitched.

Seams – sew with straight seams, using machine needle size 60–75 (9–11) depending on the base fabric with a stitch length of 2.2–2.5.

Remove sequins and beads from seam allowances by carefully cutting away individual sequins. Do not cut the threads holding them in place, as this may unravel more than you wanted.

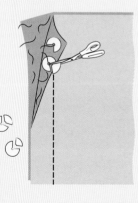

SEQUIN FABRIC

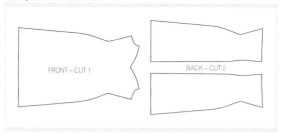

FRONT – CUT 1

BACK – CUT 2

LINING

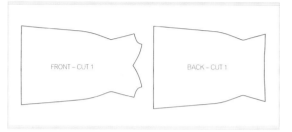

FRONT – CUT 1

BACK – CUT 1

NET

BACK YOKE

FRONT YOKE

SLEEVE – CUT 2

FRONT YOKE – CUT 1 ON FOLD
BACK YOKE – CUT 2

LAYOUT PLAN

Trace off the pattern pieces – front, back, front yoke, back yoke, sleeve. After preparing your fabric, fold it as shown on the layout plan for the width of fabric you're using and lay out the pattern pieces. Measure to the selvedge to make sure that the grain is straight. Cut out and transfer any markings to the fabric (see Get Set to Sew, page 21).

TIP

Unpin pattern pieces once all markings are transferred to the fabric but keep them folded with the fabric in case you wish to refer to them during construction.

1 MAKE UP THE YOKE

Staystitch the neck edges of the net front and back yoke pieces. With right sides together, sew the front yoke to the back yoke pieces at the shoulders with a narrow seam. (Stitch along the seam line and then stitch again with a small zigzag stitch close to the first row of stitching. Trim close to the zigzag stitching.)

2

With right sides together, stitch the back yoke pieces together at the centre seam for just 5 cm (2 in.) from the bottom edge. Press open the seam allowances. Neaten the raw edges of the back opening by turning under a double 6-mm (¼-in.) hem. Topstitch in place.

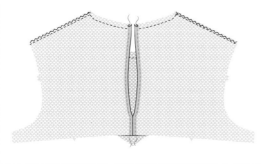

3 BIND THE NECK EDGE

Open out one long edge of the 2-cm (¾-in.) bias binding and turn the short end to the wrong side by 13 mm (½ in.). Starting at the centre back opening, placing the crease in the opened-out edge of the binding 1 cm (⅜ in.) from the neck edge, pin the binding to the WRONG side of the neckline. When you reach the other side of the neck opening, leave an extending tail of tape approximately 6.5 cm (2½ in.) for the button loop. Stitch the tape in place along the crease. Trim the seams and clip the curves.

4

Turn the bias binding to the right side of the garment, encasing the raw edge of the net yoke. At the extended tape end, pin the long edges of the tape together. Working from the right side, stitch around the very edge of the bias binding, stitching in the ditch between the net and the binding, catching the underside of the binding in place as you go. Continue to stitch along the extended tape to the end. Fold the extension into a loop and hand stitch it to the back of the neck edge.

5

Hand stitch a ball button to the opposite neck edge.

6 ATTACH THE LOWER BACK PIECES
With right sides together, pin and stitch the lower back pieces together down the centre back seam. Again with right sides together, pin and stitch the lower back to the back yoke. Press the seam down towards the sequinned lower section.

7
With right sides together, pin and stitch the lower front section to the front yoke. Press the seam down towards the sequinned lower section.

8
With right sides together, matching the side seams, pin the back to the front. Stitch the side seams from top to bottom slightly stretching the fabric as you sew.

9 INSERT THE SLEEVES
Ease stitch around the sleeve head between the notches, stitching just inside the seam allowances with a 6-mm (¼-in.) long stitch length. This will enable you to pull up the thread to fit the sleeve into the armhole later, if necessary.

10
With right sides together, matching the notches and the hem edge, stitch the side seam of the sleeve with a narrow seam (see step 1).

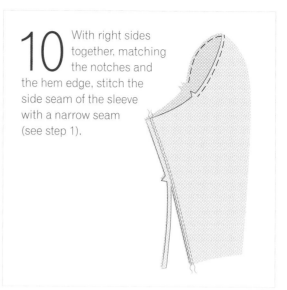

11
With right sides together, matching the top of the sleeve head to the shoulder seam of the yoke and matching the armhole seams, pin the sleeve into the armhole. If necessary, pull up a little of the ease stitching to make it fit. Note that there are notches on the sleeve but not on the yoke. The double notch on the sleeve is the back of the sleeve and the single notch is the front. Sew the sleeve in with a narrow seam (see step 1).

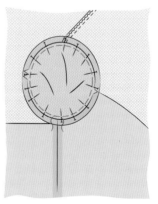

12 HEM THE SLEEVES AND DRESS
Hem the sleeves by turning under a double 6-mm (¼-in.) hem. Topstitch in place.

13 Allow the garment to hang overnight, then straighten the hem edge if necessary. With right sides together, machine stitch 2.5-cm (1-in.) bias binding to the right side of the hem edge. Turn the bias binding to the wrong side, so that the lower edge of the binding is just turned to the inside of the garment, and then slipstitch it to the inside of the garment.

14 ADD THE LINING
Insert a ballpoint or stretch needle into your machine. With right sides together, sew the back lining pieces together at the centre back seam. With right sides together again, pin the front and back lining pieces together and sew the side seams from top to bottom.

15 Turn under the top edge of the lining by 1 cm (⅜ in.). With wrong sides together, slip the dress inside the lining. Pin the top of the lining over the yoke/dress seam, effectively encasing the seam allowances, and matching the armhole lower edges. Slipstitch in place at the yoke seams on the front and back and at the armholes.

16 Turn up an 8-cm (3-in.) hem on the lining only, tucking the raw edge inside the fold to create a double-folded hem. Check that the lining is slightly shorter than the main garment and topstitch the hem in place.

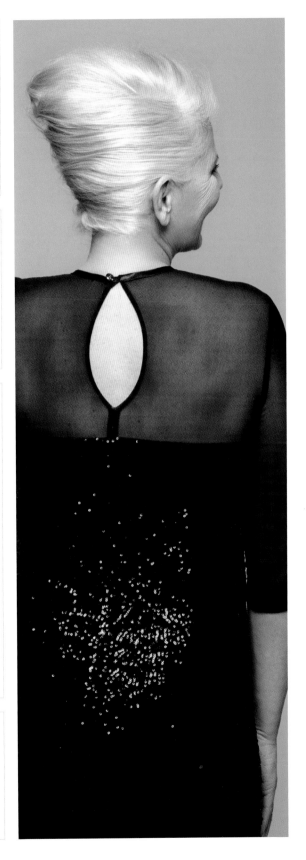

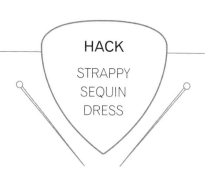

HACK

STRAPPY SEQUIN DRESS

This simple strappy dress is an excellent way to showcase a dramatic sequinned fabric. The pattern is a hack from the project on page 189, extended into an ankle-skimming length with a side split and slim straps. Choose to make your own simple fabric straps, or use ribbon.

MATERIALS

1.8–2 m of 150 cm wide (2–2 ¼ yd of 60 in.) or 3–3.2 m of 115 cm wide (3 ¼–3 ½ yd of 45 in.) stretch sequin fabric

1.8–2 m of 150 cm wide (2–2 ¼ yd of 60 in.) or 3–3.2 m of 115 cm wide (3 ¼–3 ½ yd of 45 in.) stretch lining

1.2 m (1¾ yd) fabric, bias binding or ribbon for straps, 2 cm (¾ in.) wide

Lightweight bias or knit iron-on stabilizing tape, 12 mm (½ in.) wide

Ballpoint or stretch needle

Matching sewing thread

Basic sewing kit (see page 10)

DIFFICULTY LEVEL
Intermediate

DESIGN NOTES
This elegant dress is made from three pieces of sequin fabric and a simple drop-through lining. Use 1-cm (⅜-in.) seam allowances throughout unless otherwise stated. Check the stretch of your fabric for this project: a 5-cm (2-in.) square should stretch from the grey to white area.

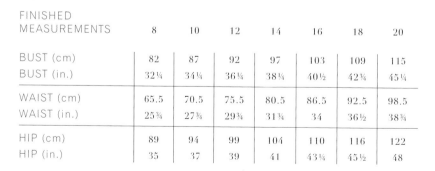

5CM OF FABRIC SHOULD STRETCH   TO AT LEAST HERE →

FINISHED MEASUREMENTS	8	10	12	14	16	18	20
BUST (cm)	82	87	92	97	103	109	115
BUST (in.)	32¼	34¼	36¼	38¼	40½	42¾	45¼
WAIST (cm)	65.5	70.5	75.5	80.5	86.5	92.5	98.5
WAIST (in.)	25¾	27¾	29¾	31¾	34	36½	38¾
HIP (cm)	89	94	99	104	110	116	122
HIP (in.)	35	37	39	41	43¼	45½	48

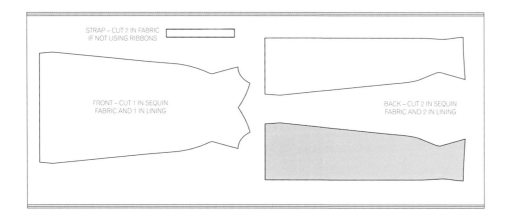

STRAP – CUT 2 IN FABRIC
IF NOT USING RIBBONS

FRONT – CUT 1 IN SEQUIN
FABRIC AND 1 IN LINING

BACK – CUT 2 IN SEQUIN
FABRIC AND 2 IN LINING

LAYOUT PLAN

Trace off the pattern pieces – front, back, and straps if you're not using bias binding or ribbon – using the longer cutting line option for the dress. After preparing your fabric, fold it as shown on the layout and lay out the pattern pieces. Measure to the selvedge to ensure the grain is straight. Cut out and transfer any markings to the fabric (see Get Set to Sew, page 21).

ADJUST THE PATTERN PIECES

The sequin dress pattern was designed for sleeves, so the front needs to be adjusted to make it more like a strappy vest top. Measure and mark a point 5 cm (2 in.) down from the tip of the front edge. Using a curved ruler, draw a new underarm seam line from the marked point to the original underarm, as indicated by the solid line. Cut out your pattern along this new shaped line.

1 MAKE UP THE DRESS

With right sides together, pin and stitch the two back pieces together at the centre back seam. Press the seam to one side.

2

Apply a strip of lightweight knit interfacing to the wrong side of the top edge of the back to stabilise it.

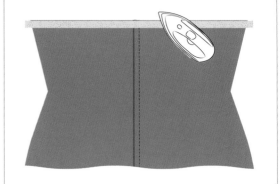

3

Staystitch (see page 29) the top edges of the dress front, stitching 1 cm (⅜ in.) from the edge. As there is a slight curve at the front of the bodice and a V-neck, sew slowly, making sure you don't stretch the fabric.

4 Apply a strip of lightweight knit interfacing to wrong side of the neckline and armhole of the front dress piece.

5 With right sides together, pin and stitch the front to the back at the side seams, sewing the right side only to the marked point for the side slit and the left side along the whole length of the seam. Press the seam allowances open.

6 MAKE UP THE LINING
Insert a ballpoint or stretch needle into your machine and repeat steps 1–5 with the lining pieces, excluding the interfacing, this time sew the right seam the whole length and the left seam to the marked point. (When turned the dress is turned right side out, the slit will be on the right side, in line with the dress slit.)

TIP

Pin the straps into position on the sequin dress, and try it on. This allows you to adjust the length of the straps before you stitch them into the lining.

7 MAKE UP AND ATTACH THE STRAPS
Insert a universal needle into your machine. If you are making fabric strips, fold the strap pieces in half lengthways, right sides together. Pin and then sew along the length with a 1.5-cm (⅝-in.) seam allowance. Turn right side out and roll so that the seam is in the centre. Press flat.

TIP

It's really worth taking your time to clip into seam allowances, as this allows the lining to sit smoothly inside the dress. Take your time and don't go closer than 2 mm (a scant ⅛ in.) to the stitching as you clip.

8 Pin and stitch the straps to the RIGHT side of the front peaks of the dress, with the raw edges even and the straps hanging downwards. Once stitched, loop the straps over to the back of the dress and pin in place, approximately 5 cm (2 in.) from the centre back seam only. Try on the dress and adjust the length of the straps at the back to suit. Make sure you haven't twisted the straps, and then machine across them with a 1-cm (⅜-in.) seam allowance.

9 **FINISH THE DRESS**
With right sides together, matching the side seams and the notches along the upper edge, slide the lining over the top of the dress. Pin and sew around the neckline and armholes, taking care to pivot precisely at the centre of the V-neck. Snip into the V at the centre front, close to but not through the stitching. Trim off the top of the points. Clip into the curved areas around the top of the bodice.

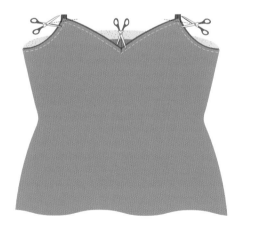

10 Press the lining and seam allowances away from the bodice and understitch as far as you can on the lining, close to the seam line, catching the seam allowances underneath. Because of the points, you won't be able to go all the way around.

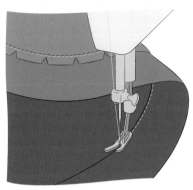

11 Allow the garment to hang overnight and then, if necessary, straighten the hem edge. With right sides together, machine stitch bias binding to the right side of the hem edge. Turn up the bias binding to the wrong side, so the lower edge of the binding is just turned to the inside of the garment, and then slipstitch it to the inside of the garment.

12 Turn up an 8-cm (3-in.) hem on the lining, tucking the raw edge inside the fold to create a double-folded hem and topstitch in place.

13 Slipstitch the slit opening of the lining to the main fabric to hold the layers together.

CAMISOLE TOP & SHORTS

CAMISOLE TOP & SHORTS

A lace-trimmed camisole is so versatile. Right now it is fashionable to wear lingerie-style garments as fashion wear, but of course this top can also be made as loungewear or nightwear. Whatever your preference, make it in a silky, soft fabric for a luxurious feel. French seams and tiny shoulder straps give a professional finish. The lace-trimmed shorts complement them perfectly.

MATERIALS FOR TOP
1 m (1 yd) fabric, 115–150 cm (45–60 in.) wide

1.5 m (1⅝ yd) lace trim, 38 mm (1½ in.) wide

50 cm (20 in.) lingerie (plush back) elastic, 1 cm (⅜ in.) wide

2 x ribbon roses or bows (optional)

Matching sewing thread

Loop turner or hair grip

Basic sewing kit (see page 10)

MATERIALS FOR SHORTS
40 cm (16 in.) cotton lawn, silky satin or crepe de chine, 115–150 cm (45–60 in.) wide

1 m (1 yd) lace trim, 38 mm (1½ in.) wide

1.1 m (1¼ yd) elastic, 20 mm (¾ in.) wide

Matching sewing thread

Basic sewing kit (see page 10)

DIFFICULTY LEVEL
Intermediate

FABRIC SUGGESTIONS
Cotton lawn, silk, lingerie satin, crepe de chine.

DESIGN NOTES
This simple design gives you the opportunity to practise lots of skills, including narrow straps, French seams and lace application. The straps on the camisole top are cut on the bias, as they will be more comfortable to wear.

Use a 1.5-cm (⅝-in.) seam allowance throughout, unless otherwise stated.

CAMISOLE TOP

FINISHED SHORTS MEASUREMENTS	8	10	12	14	16	18	20
BUST (cm)	88	93	98	103	109	115	121
BUST (in.)	34½	36½	38½	40½	43	45¼	47½
WAIST (cm)	94	99	104	109	115	121	127
WAIST (in.)	37	39	41	43	45¼	47½	50

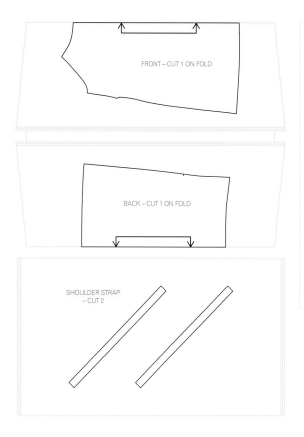

FRONT – CUT 1 ON FOLD

BACK – CUT 1 ON FOLD

SHOULDER STRAP – CUT 2

LAYOUT PLAN

Trace off the pattern pieces – back, front, shoulder strap and elastic guide. After preparing your fabric, fold the selvedges in to the middle, right sides together, and measure to the selvedges to make sure that the grain is straight. For the shoulder straps, lay the fabric out in a single layer and cut out the strap twice. Cut out and transfer any markings to the fabric (see Get Set to Sew, page 21). Note that the elastic guide is not cut out of fabric; it is just there for you to measure your elastic against.

1 STITCH THE BUST DARTS

Fold the bust darts on the front by folding the fabric right sides together, matching the dart markings. Tack and stitch from the side seam, tapering to the fold of the fabric at the tip and taking the last two or three stitches right on the fold. Do not backstitch; instead, leave thread tails and tie off the ends. Press the bust darts over a ham (see Darts, page 150). Press the darts downwards.

2 ADD THE LACE TRIM

Lay the front flat, right side up. Pin the lace trim to the upper edge, placing the outer edge of the lace along the raw edge of the fabric, as shown, and folding in the fullness at the corners. Stitch along the lower edge of the lace, using a zigzag stitch (width 2.5, length 1.5).

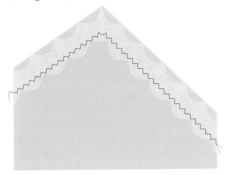

3

Turn the piece over and trim away the fabric just below the stitching to reveal the lace, taking care not to cut into the lace.

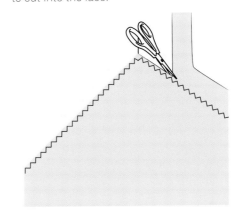

4 ELASTICATE THE BACK

Cut a piece of 1-cm (⅜-in.) elastic using the elastic guide.

5

Pin the elastic to the upper edge of the back, on the right side, placing one long edge along the raw edge of the back and stretching the elastic slightly so that it fits the back. Stitch 6 mm (¼ in.) from the upper edge, using straight stitch and stretching the fabric and elastic slightly as you stitch.

6

Turn the elastic to the wrong side of the back along the seam and press. Stitch close to the upper edge, using stretch 3-step zigzag stitch, again stretching the elastic slightly as you stitch.

7

STITCH THE FRONT TO THE BACK
Stitch the side seams using a French seam (see page 42) to encase the raw edges of the seam allowance. Press the seams towards the back.

8

ATTACH THE STRAPS
Fold the strap in half lengthways, right sides together, and stitch using a 6-mm (¼-in.) seam allowance. To turn the strap, cut a small snip on the fold 1 cm (⅜ in.) from one end. Thread the strap onto the loop turner and place the end of the strap up to the snip into the latch of the loop turner. Pull the loop turner back through the strap. Trim the end. Alternatively, use a hair grip, hook the pin through the snipped opening, insert it into the strap and guide it through to the other end. Repeat for the second strap.

9

Pin one end of each strap to the wrong side of the front, centring it over the folds in the lace. Turn under 6 mm (¼ in.) on the end and stitch to the front fabric by hand. Secure the strap to the lace with a hand stitch.

10

Try the camisole on and adjust the strap length. Turn under 6 mm (¼ in.) on the unstitched end of each strap and stitch to the back by hand.

11 On the right side of the camisole, starting at one side seam, pin the lace trim to the lower edge, as in step 2. Turn under 6 mm (¼ in.) on each end of the lace at the side seam. Stitch close to the upper edge of the lace, using a straight or a zigzag stitch (width 2.5, length 1.5).

12 Turn the piece over and trim away the fabric just below the stitching to reveal the lace, as in step 3, taking care not to cut into the lace. Slipstitch the ends of the lace together.

13 If you wish, attach two ribbon roses or bows to the front where the straps meet the lace.

TIP

When working with silky fabrics, do not fold the fabric when cutting as it tends to slip. Lay the fabric out in a single layer and pin the pattern pieces in place (with the grain straight). Cut one of each piece, then flip the pattern over and repeat.

CORE SKILL
Sewing with lace

SEAMS

To prevent snags or puckers, hold the lace fabric taut when sewing, feeding it through gently. If it still seems to snag, place a little tissue paper under the seamline, which can then be torn away after stitching. Use a narrow double-stitched seam to minimise the seam allowance show through, or use a satin binding to make a feature of them.

TIPS

- When working with a commercial pattern, check the fabric suggestions to see whether lace is suitable as a fabric choice. Even if it is not listed, it can be used as a trim or inserted. Select simple designs with few pattern pieces, as these will work best and will not detract from the fabric.
- Make all pattern adjustments prior to laying out the pattern on the fabric.
- Some laces have a definite 'one-way' design with a right way up. Follow the 'with nap' layout to make sure that all pattern pieces are placed in the right direction.
- Prevent the fabric being pulled into the feed dogs by using a straight stitch throat plate on your machine, if available. Alternatively, place tape on either side of the needle hole to make it smaller.
- Avoid backstitching to prevent jamming. Hold the thread ends as you begin, and tie them together to finish.

NARROW DOUBLE-STITCHED SEAM

Stitch a plain seam, then stitch again 3 mm (⅛ in.) away in the seam allowance, using a straight or zigzag stitch. Trim close to the second stitching. Press the seam to one side. If darts are to be made, use the double-stitched method, trimming the dart fold close to the stitching.

BOUND SEAMS

Stitch a plain seam and then trim the seam allowance to 6 mm (¼ in.). Press both seam allowances together to one side. Wrap a narrow bias binding around the seam allowances only and stitch.

HEMS

Lace can be left unhemmed but if a hem is required, take a narrow double-turned hem, turning up just 1 cm (⅜ in.), tucking the raw edge inside and slipstitching or machine topstitching. When using a scallop-edged lace, cut the pattern with the scallop edge at the hem (on a straight-hemmed garment). Remember to deduct the hem allowance from the length of the pattern piece. With a curved hem, the scallop can be used, but cut off the fabric and then stitch on top of the lace at the hemline, around the top edge of the trim, allowing the scallop to hang below. Trim away the lace from the garment under the scallop.

SHORTS

FINISHED SHORTS MEASUREMENTS	8	10	12	14	16	18	20
WAIST (cm)	96	101	106	111	117	123	129
WAIST (in.)	37¾	39¾	41¾	43¾	46	48½	50¾

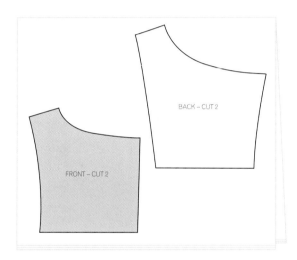

BACK – CUT 2

FRONT – CUT 2

LAYOUT PLAN

Trace off the pattern pieces – front and back. After preparing your fabric, fold it in half, right sides together, and lay out the pattern pieces as shown. Place pieces shown in grey face down. Measure to the selvedge to make sure that the grain is straight. Cut out and transfer any markings to the fabric (see Get Set to Sew, page 21).

1 Stitch a front and a back piece together along the side seam, using a French seam (see page 42). Press the seam towards the back.

2 **ATTACH THE LACE TRIM**
Open out the joined front and back piece and lay it flat, right side up. Pin the wrong side of the lace trim to the lower edge, placing the lower edge of the lace along the raw edge of the shorts. Stitch along the upper edge of the lace with a zigzag stitch (width 2.5, length 1.5).

3 Turn the piece over and trim away the fabric below the stitching to reveal the lace, taking care not to cut into the lace.

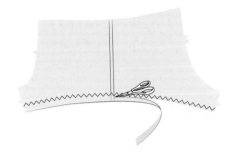

4 STITCH THE INSIDE LEG SEAM
Stitch the front and back together at the inside leg, using a French seam as before. Press the seam towards the back, as in step 1. Repeat steps 1–4 for the other leg.

5 STITCH THE CROTCH SEAM
With wrong sides together, matching the side seams and notches, place one leg inside the other and pin and stitch the crotch seam. Trim the seam allowance to a scant 3 mm (⅛ in.) and turn through so that the right sides are together. Stitch again to complete the French seam. Press the seam to one side.

6 ELASTICATE THE WAIST
To form the casing for the elastic, turn the upper edge to the inside along the fold line, turning under 6 mm (¼ in.) on the raw edge. Press. Stitch close to the upper and lower edges of the casing, leaving a gap in the lower stitching to insert the elastic.

7 Cut the elastic to the measurement of your waist plus 2.5 cm (1 in.). Attach a safety pin to one end of the elastic and feed it through the casing. Overlap the ends and secure with the safety pin. Try on and adjust the elastic to fit.

8 Stitch the ends of the elastic securely together. Allow the elastic to slip inside the casing and then slipstitch the opening closed.

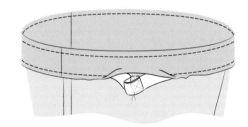

MEN'S PIN-TUCK SHIRT

MEN'S PIN-TUCK SHIRT

Every man should own a classic dress shirt: it's an iconic piece of clothing that has been part of every wardrobe since the 19th century. Our dress shirt has a twist on the plain front, with a band of vertical pin tucks adding an interesting style detail.

MATERIALS
2.5 m (2¾ yd) fabric, 150 cm (60 in.) wide

25 cm (10 in.) iron-on interfacing to match the weight of your fabric

9 buttons, 8–13 mm (approx. ⅜–½ in.) in diameter

Matching sewing thread

Twin needle

Pin tuck foot

Buttonhole foot

Basic sewing kit (see page 10)

DIFFICULTY LEVEL
Intermediate/Advanced

FABRIC SUGGESTIONS
Cotton, shirting, linen, linen blend, poplin.

DESIGN NOTES
This shirt is a combination of many techniques and pieces, including a stand collar, sleeve plackets, buttonholes and pin tucks. The pin tucks are made with a twin needle and a pin tuck foot. The collar and cuffs are interfaced. Perfect buttonholes are sewn by machine with a buttonhole foot.

Use a 1.5-cm (⅝-in.) seam allowance throughout, unless otherwise stated.

FINISHED MEASUREMENTS	36	38	40	42	44	46	48
CHEST (cm)	101.5	107.25	110.5	113.5	116.75	123	125.75
CHEST (in.)	40	42¼	43½	44¾	46	48¼	49½

CORE SKILL
Simple pin tucking techniques

Narrow pin tucks create a subtle surface detail that adds a distinct designer feel to a garment. Often used on heirloom garments, especially children's clothes and christening gowns, they also look smart on crisp, formal shirts and blouses. They are most effective when stitched in multiple pin tuck groups.

TWIN NEEDLE PIN TUCKS

1 Insert a twin needle with gap of 2 mm (⅛ in.). Select a straight stitch, with the needle in the centre position. Increase the top tension to the highest (7–9) and use a stitch length of 2. Attach the pin tuck foot. Thread the machine for twin needle sewing, following the instructions in your sewing machine manual.

2 Mark the fabric for the placement of the first row of pin tucks. Stitch the first row with the centre of the pin tuck foot on the marked line.

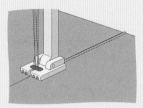

TIP

Make sure that the first row is perfectly straight, as this determines the accuracy of the following rows.

3 Having stitched the first tuck, move the fabric so that the first tuck runs in one of the grooves on either side of the centre of the foot, so that the next tuck is perfectly parallel to the first. Stitch all the tucks in the same direction.

SEWING PIN TUCKS WITHOUT A SPECIALIST FOOT OR TWIN NEEDLE

Pin tucks can be sewn without specialist tools – you just need to take more care in marking the tuck positions and ensure they are stitched accurately.

If you are using a commercial pattern, the tucks will be marked on the pattern pieces. Transfer these markings to the right side of the fabric at the seam edge, using a different pin or chalk colour to determine which is the fold line and which is the stitching line.

1 If you are making your own, determine the depth of the finished tuck and multiply by three. Also allow a gap

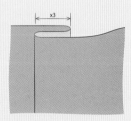

between tucks – the width is up to you. With these two measurements added together, mark the fold lines on the fabric at top and bottom by snipping into the seam allowance or using pins.

2 Fold the fabric along the fold line from top to bottom, with wrong sides together, and press to make a firm crease.

3 Place the fabric under the presser foot, and stitch a straight line the tuck depth required from the fold.

4 Unfold the tucked fabric and then refold to stitch the next tuck in the same manner. Always press in the fold first to make sure they are stitched in straight rows.

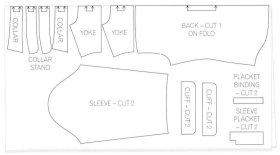

LAYOUT PLAN

Trace off the pattern pieces – back, yoke, collar, collar stand, sleeve, sleeve placket, placket binding, cuff and left and right fronts. After preparing your fabric, fold the fabric in half widthways, right sides together, and lay out all the pattern pieces, except the left and right fronts, as shown. Measure to the selvedge to make sure that the grain is straight. Lay out the front pieces in a single layer. Cut out and transfer any markings to the fabric (see Get Set to Sew, page 21).

1 Apply iron-on interfacing to the wrong side of one collar piece, one collar stand piece and two cuff pieces. Apply a 2.7-cm (1¹⁄₁₆-in.) strip of interfacing to the centre front edge of the left front and a 2-cm (¾-in.) strip of interfacing to the centre front edge of the right front.

2 MAKE THE SLEEVE PLACKETS
Fold under 1 cm (⅜ in.) to the wrong side on one long side of each sleeve placket and placket binding piece, as shown, and press. Fold under and press the top edge of each sleeve placket piece by 1 cm (⅜ in.), too.

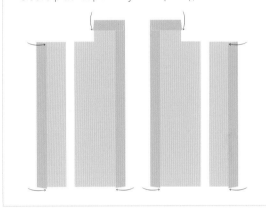

TIP

Make sure to make a mirrored set!

TIP

If you're matching a pattern, cut one of the shirt fronts first, right side up, and then place it right side down to find where the pattern for the second shirt front will match.

CORE SKILL
Beautiful buttonholes

Modern machines will either sew a buttonhole in one step or, on basic models, in four steps. Many now come with a buttonhole foot with a slot in the back for the button, so that the hole is the perfect size.

BUTTONHOLE SIZE

If your machine does not have a foot that fits a button in the back, work out buttonhole size, measure flat buttons across the width and add 3 mm (⅛ in.). For domed buttons, measure the circumference and add 3 mm (⅛ in.).

POSITIONING BUTTONHOLES

Buttonholes should be a minimum of 1–2 cm (⅜–¾ in.) from the fabric edge, and 5–8 cm (2–3 in.) apart, depending on the fabric weight and the style of the garment.

STITCHING A BUTTONHOLE

Prepare the fabric by interfacing the buttonhole section. On very lightweight fabrics, add an extra layer of tearaway stabiliser below each buttonhole area. Mark the buttonhole positions.

BUTTONHOLE FOOT WITH SLOT FOR BUTTON

1 Insert the button into the back of the foot, following the manufacturer's instructions.

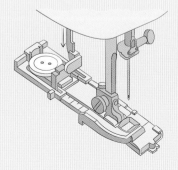

2 Snap on the buttonhole foot and bring down the buttonhole lever. Set the sewing machine to your chosen buttonhole stitch, which is usually a one-step buttonhole when this foot is supplied.

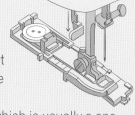

3 Position the garment under the foot, with the needle ready to insert into the correct end of buttonhole placement mark (which end of buttonhole depends on which way your machine stitches). Once stitched, feed the thread tails through to the back of the work and then through the close stitching of one side before cutting off.

4 Use the sharp seam ripper (quick unpick) to open the buttonhole, placing a pin at one end and starting at the other.

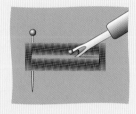

FOUR-STEP BUTTONHOLE

1 Prepare the fabric and mark the buttonhole position as above.

2 Attach the buttonhole foot and select step 1 of the buttonhole sequence. (You may need to adjust the stitch length down to virtually 0, too.) Stitch the first end bar tack. Once complete, the machine will stop ready for you to turn the dial to step 2 to stitch the left side of the buttonhole.

3 Stitch the length needed, stopping at the chalk line made for your buttonhole size. Turn the dial back to step 1 for the second bar tack. Then turn the dial to stitch the right-hand side, stitching until you reach the first bar tack. Take threads to the back and tie off. Open the buttonhole, as above.

3 Lay the sleeves out, wrong side up, and cut the marked opening on each one. Place the placket pieces and placket bindings wrong side up on each side of the slit, aligning the raw edges and remembering to mirror their positions on the second sleeve. Pin in place and stitch along each side to the top of the slit, using a 1-cm (⅜-in.) seam allowance. Cut from the top of the split towards either side of the stitched edges to form a Y-shape.

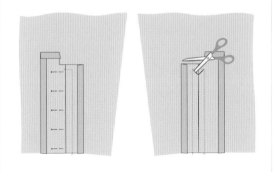

4 Turn the placket piece through the stitching/slash line onto the right side of the sleeve. Wrap the placket binding around the raw edge of that side of the slit, encasing the stitching. Press, pin and topstitch in place close to the original seamline.

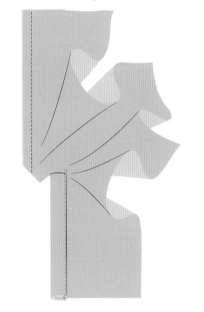

5 Fold the sleeve placket in half, wrong sides together, making sure you cover the line of stitching, and press. Pin in place, including the free edge of the overlap, and topstitch, starting at the hem edge.

6 MAKE THE PIN TUCKS

Insert a twin needle and pin tuck foot into your sewing machine. Referring to your manual, thread your sewing machine with two spools of thread. Transfer the position of your first pin tuck from the pattern. Following the instructions on page 212, line up the marked line in the middle of the twin needles and, working from top to bottom, stitch the first tuck. Sew your second pin tuck by positioning the completed tuck in the next groove of the pin tuck foot, either to the right or left. (This will depend on which side of the shirt you're working on.) Repeat until you've stitched six rows of pin tucks on both shirt fronts.

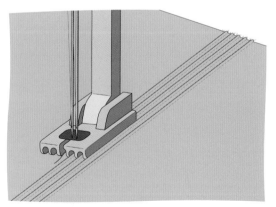

7 MAKE THE BUTTON STANDS

On the left front of the shirt (as worn), fold the centre front edge to the wrong side by 2.7 cm (1⅛ in.) and press. Topstitch 2 mm (a scant ⅛ in.) from the fold. Fold over another 2.7 cm (1¹⁄₁₆ in.), press and topstitch 2 mm (a scant ⅛ in.) from the fold, catching the raw centre front edge in the stitching. Open out the flap and press flat.

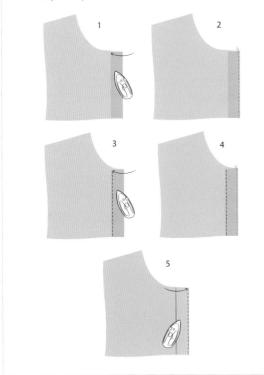

8

On the right front of the shirt (as worn), fold the centre front edge to the wrong side by 2 cm (¾ in.) and press, then fold over another 2 cm (¾ in.) and press again. Topstitch close to the inside fold.

9 ATTACH THE YOKE

Matching up the centre back notches, pin the right side of the inner yoke to the wrong side of the shirt back along the top edge. Machine stitch, using a 13-mm (½-in.) seam allowance. With right sides together, pin the outer yoke on top of the shirt back. The shirt back is now sandwiched between the two yoke layers. Machine in place with a 1.5-cm (⅝-in.) seam allowance.

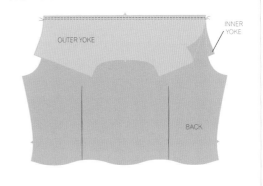

OUTER YOKE

INNER YOKE

BACK

10 With right sides together, pin both shirt fronts to the outer yoke at the shoulder seams and machine with a 13-mm seam (½-in.) allowance. Lay the shirt flat onto a table so that the two yoke layers are opened out, with the right sides facing up. Roll the shirt back into a small tube onto the inner yoke. Then roll the two shirt fronts into small tubes, towards and onto the outer yoke.

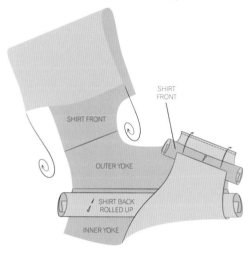

SHIRT FRONT

SHIRT FRONT

OUTER YOKE

SHIRT BACK ROLLED UP

INNER YOKE

11 Pick up the corner of the inner yoke, and fold it over the rolled tubes. Pin at the shoulder seams. The shirt body pieces are now sandwiched inside and between the yoke panels. Machine the shoulder seams with a 1.5-cm (⅝-in.) seam allowance.

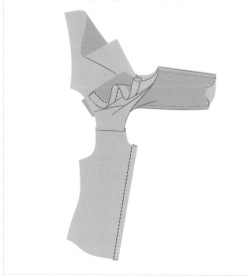

12 Pull the front and back pieces through one of the side openings. The seams are neatly hidden inside the yoke. Press all seams flat. Working from the right side, topstitch 2 mm (a scant ⅛ in.) on the front and back shoulder seams. Then staystitch the neck and armhole edges 6 mm (¼ in.) from the raw edge to stabilise.

13 **ATTACH THE SLEEVES**
With right sides together, matching the notches, lay the armhole over the sleeve head. Pin and machine. Neaten the raw edge with a zigzag stitch or an overlocker. Press the seam allowance towards the body, then topstitch the armhole from the right side.

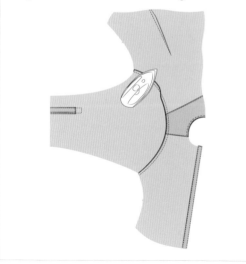

14 Fold the shirt right sides together, and pin and sew the front to the back along the underarm and side seams, making sure to match up the underarm seams and all notches. Neaten the raw edges with a zigzag stitch or an overlocker.

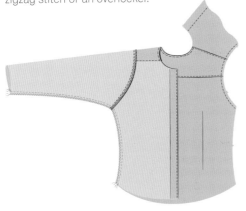

TIP

Alternatively, you can flat fell both the armhole and the side seams (see page 42); there's a really useful flat fell foot available for most domestic sewing machines.

15 ADD THE CUFFS
Fold the pleats on the sleeve edges, as marked. Tack in place close to the raw edge.

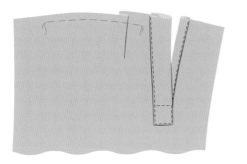

16 Along one long edge of one cuff piece, press 1 cm (⅜ in.) to the wrong side. With right sides together, pin and stitch a second cuff piece to the first around the curved upper edge and short sides. Notch the curved edge and turn right side out. Repeat for the other cuff.

17 Pin the un-pressed edge of the cuff to the shirt sleeve, with the right side of the cuff facing the wrong side of the sleeve and making sure 1.5 cm (⅝ in.) of the cuff extends beyond each side of the placket pieces. Machine with a 1-cm (⅜-in.) seam allowance.

18 With right sides together, fold the cuff in half along its length and line up the short ends. The pressed edge should sit just below the seam joining the cuff to the sleeve. Machine stitch the short ends with a 1-cm (⅜-in.) seam allowance.

19 Turn the cuff to the right side and topstitch in place, sandwiching the seam allowance between the layers. Topstitch all around the outer edges of the cuff.

20 MAKE THE COLLAR
Press the seam allowance to the wrong side along the bottom edge of the inner collar stand. Pin the collar pieces right sides together and sew around the outer edges. Trim and grade the corners to get a good point. Turn through and press well. Machine baste the open inner edge.

21 Pin the wrong side of the collar to the right side of the un-pressed outer collar stand and machine stitch. Place the inner collar stand over the top, right side down, so that the collar is sandwiched in between the collar stand pieces, and sew around the collar stand edge.

INNER COLLAR STAND
OUTER COLLAR STAND
COLLAR

22 With right sides together, matching all notches, pin and then stitch the inside collar around the neckline.

23 Pin the inside edge of the collar to the neckline and topstitch around the collar stand.

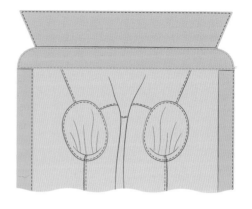

24 HEM THE SHIRT
Turn under and press 6 mm (¼ in.) to the wrong side along the shirt hem. Make a second 1-cm (⅜-in.) fold, press in place, then topstitch along the inside folded edge.

TIP
You can buy a narrow rolled hem foot attachment for most domestic sewing machines that works well for narrow hems.

25 MAKE THE BUTTONHOLES
Following the instructions on page 214, mark the buttonholes on the left shirt front, spacing them evenly. Sew and cut open the buttonholes. Sew the buttons to the button stand on the right shirt front. Give the shirt a final press.

INDEX

ACKNOWLEDGEMENTS

LOVE PRODUCTIONS would like to thank the viewers who watch The Great British Sewing Bee, especially those who have felt inspired enough to buy this book. It is the perfect accompaniment to the series thanks to the expertise of author, Wendy Gardiner, and the dedication of the team at Quadrille, Lisa Pendreigh, Helen Lewis and Emily Lapworth. The clever people behind the design, Susanna Cook, Nikki Dupin and Andie Redman have once again helped to produce a truly covetable book. It is a real privilege to work on The Great British Sewing Bee and get to know the brilliant sewers behind the gorgeous garments: Angeline, Charlotte, Duncan, Ghislaine, Jade, Jamie, Josh, Joyce, Rumana and Tracey, you are all amazing. We would like to thank the judges; the arbiter of good taste, Patrick Grant and the inspirational Esme Young for everything they have taught us about what home sewers should aspire to make. A big thank you to our ball of energy of a host, Claudia Winkleman, who has kept us entertained throughout. For commissioning a fourth series and for all their support, we would like to thank the BBC, particularly Donna Clark and Catherine Catton. A final word has to go to the very talented, hardworking team who work behind the scenes on the show. It is their passion and drive that ensures *The Great British Sewing Bee* is the best series it can be… and a nicer bunch of people you could not hope to meet.

WENDY GARDINER would like to thank *The Great British Sewing Bee* team from Love Productions, Stuart Cooper of Metrostar Media and Lisa Pendreigh from Quadrille for inviting me to write this iconic book. Particular thanks go to Claire-Louise Hardie, Rachel Farrimond and Fiona Parker whose incredible hard work on the Bee didn't stop them from being an enormous help to me with all the garments, patterns and instructions from the series included in the book, as well as sourcing all the fabrics used throughout. Thanks also to Susanne Rock and Anna Driver from Love Productions who were always so welcoming. Thanks to Eddie at The Sampling Studio and Zuhair at Gradehouse for their expert work on pattern cutting and pattern grading. A very particular thanks to Claire Tyler, a fellow tutor and sewing expert whose help with some of the projects proved invaluable. Without her by my side, this book may never have been written in time. Finally thanks to the editing team, Sarah Hoggett and Helen Rochester, the illustrators, Stephen Dew, Suzie London and Kate Simunek, and designer Emily Lapworth whose tireless work has helped to create this beautiful book of which we can all be proud.

This book is published to accompany the television series entitled *The Great British Sewing Bee*, first broadcast on BBC TWO in 2016.

Executive Producers Richard McKerrow, Anna Beattie & Susanne Rock
Series Producer James Hedge
Series Director Jeanette Goulbourn
Senior Casting Producer Anna Driver
Producer Victoria Howarth
Casting Producer Rosie Geiger
Sewing Producer Claire-Louise Hardie
Sewing Assistants Rachel Farrimond, Fiona Parker & Chloe Holdforth
Production Executive Fin O'Riordan
Unit Manager Helen Robson
Production Manager Eleanore Sharpe
Director of Legal & Commercial Affairs Rupert Frisby
Publicity Amanda Console & Shelagh Pymm
BBC Commissioning Executive Catherine Catton
BBC Head of Formats & Features Donna Clark

First published in 2016 by
Quadrille Publishing Ltd
Pentagon House
52–54 Southwark Street
London SE1 1UN
www.quadrille.co.uk

Quadrille is an imprint of Hardie Grant
www.hardiegrant.com.au

Publishing Director Sarah Lavelle
Commissioning Editor Lisa Pendreigh
Project Editors Sarah Hoggett & Helen Rochester
Garment Designers Jasmine Carey, Wendy Gardiner, Susan Goodwin, Claire-Louise Hardie, Lynda Kinne & Claire Tyler
Pattern Cutters Zuhair Alzahr, Jasmine Carey, Susan Goodwin, Eddie Gavriilidis, Claire-Louise Hardie, Lynda Kinne & Claire Tyler
Garment Makers Zuhair Alzahr, Jasmine Carey, Rachel Farrimond, Melissa Fehr, Rachel Frost, Susan Goodwin, Eddie Gavriilidis, Claire-Louise Hardie & Lynda Kinne
Pattern Grading Gradehouse
Creative Director Helen Lewis
Book Design Concept and Creative Direction Susanna Cook and Allies Design Studio
Book Design Emily Lapworth
Book Design Assistant Gemma Hayden
Illustrators Kate Simunek, Stephen Dew & Suzie London
Photographers Jenni Hare & Charlotte Medlicott
Photoshoot Production and Art Direction nicandlou
Stylist Andie Redman
Hair and Make-up Nicky Tavilla
Models Rebecca & Zvona at Bookings; Shenyue at Models 1; Lise & Mimi at Nevs; David at Premier; Barnaby, Freya, Rosabelle & Seren
Production Director Vincent Smith
Production Controller Emily Noto

British Library Cataloguing-in-Publication Data
A catalogue record for this book is available from the British Library.

ISBN 978 184949 882 1

10 9 8 7 6 5 4 3 2 1

Printed and bound in Italy.

If you have any comments or queries regarding the instructions in this book, please contact us at enquiries@quadrille.co.uk.

MALP 26/6/16